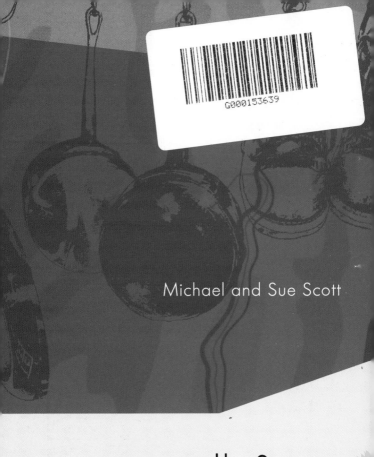

Michael and Sue Scott

walk & eat
CAPE TOWN

CONTENTS

Cape Town, a dynamic, modern, cosmopolitan city, is well-blessed for walkers, with Table Mountain and Lion's Head on its doorstep, and the rugged Cape Peninsula just a short trip away by public transport. With excellent restaurants, glorious weather most of the year, and daily flights from major airports, it makes a perfect holiday destination.

This guide contains enough walks, excursions, restaurants and recipes to occupy most of two weeks, so you can chose whichever appeal to you most. The highlights at a glance:

- 12 varied day walks, each with topographical map
- 2 excursions, each providing access to some walks
- recommended restaurants linked to each walk
- recipes using the best of South African produce, to make at your self-catering base (and perhaps back home)
- special section with hints on wheat-, gluten- and dairy-free eating and cooking in Cape Town

INTRO

THE EXCURSIONS

Books in the *walk & eat* series are based around public transport, for those who prefer not to drive. In Cape Town, some buses and trains are not recommended for visitors (see page 14). However, we've chosen two short excursions, one by train and one by tourist bus, on which visitors are welcomed and safe.

The bus trip circumnavigates Table Mountain, via Kirstenbosch Botanic Gardens, Constantia Nek and Hout Bay, from each of which we also recommend walks. The train travels down the Cape Peninsula as far as Simon's Town, and provides access to several other walks and on to Cape Point itself. Even if you don't do the walks, the excursions are well worth taking for an overview of the area's landscapes.

THE WALKS

Here, we were spoilt for choice. We've consulted friends and local experts to select the best walks around Cape Town. We've tried them all ourselves, and selected our favourites. These are *not* walks for fanatical hikers, although some are fairly demanding. In our view, there is no point in travelling to Cape Town *just* to walk. Rather, we hope that readers will want to take the time to explore and to *look*. Our walks are designed to be enjoyed at leisure, and to give a feel for the culture, landscapes and some of the wildlife of the Cape Peninsula.

The walks range from an easy stroll in Simon's Town taking in a beach full of African penguins to a rugged climb onto the Lion's Head for a stunning view. They include the best walks on

Wildlife, like these African black oystercatchers, are a strong feature of all our walks.

Table Mountain, and a selection of great walks on the Cape Peninsula, from Muizenberg to Cape Point.

THE RESTAURANTS

Food should be a highlight of any holiday, and the food in Cape Town is almost uniformly good and rarely expensive. We've selected restaurants that combine with our walks, providing a memorable end to a wonderful ramble, a relaxing lunch *en route*, or a wholesome breakfast before you start. We've chosen restaurants that specialise in South African or Cape Malay food, so you can enjoy real Cape Town eating.

We had two key tests for the restaurant. Firstly, they had to welcome us straight off the hill, hot, scruffy and tired. Secondly, the staff (often called 'waitrons' in politically correct Cape Town) had to be able to cope with Sue's 'difficult' diet, so we can guarantee that every restaurant in the book can provide gluten- and dairy-free meals if you ask. We chose all the restaurants before telling them we were researching a book, and *no restaurant has paid, in cash or kind, to be included in this guide.*

There is plenty of accommodation available from Muizenberg to Simon's Town and at Hout Bay if you want to extend your stay and not worry about late-night transport: book ahead with Cape Town Tourism (see page 18).

All our recommended restaurants are good value by European standards. They are all broadly in the same price range, but we've attempted a rough price code for each (see box). Booking ahead for these restaurants is rarely needed, but it's worth considering if you are planning your walk to include a meal! Many have web sites, with photographs to whet your appetite!

KEY TO THE RESTAURANT ENTRIES
(telephone number; www. web site; @ e-mail address
R = main meal under R100*
RR = main meal R100–130*
RRR = main meal over R130*
CC: credit cards accepted: Visa (**V**), Mastercard (**MC**), American Express (**AM**), Diners Club (**DC**)
*based on starter, main course and coffee, including any cover charges

THE RECIPES

Some days, after a long walk, it is much nicer to 'eat in' at your apartment. We've asked our friends in Cape Town, and some of the restaurants we've visited, for recipes based on fresh, local South African produce and suited for self-catering apartments. We've

'Café' usually conjures up formica table-tops, ketchup bottles and so-so food. Not so in the Cape! Yes, the atmosphere is casual, and the décor anything but elegant, *but* the quality of the food is very high. Examples are this gorgonzola sirloin at the Olympia Café in Kalk Bay — or the superb and imaginative dishes at the Café Paradiso in Cape Town (page 42) and the Empire Café in Muizenberg (page 120).

tried them all ourselves in the apartments we've stayed in, to make sure they work with an oven, a couple of rings and a limited range of dishes and utensils.

South Africans love their *braais* (barbecues), and many apartments in rural areas have a *braai* in the garden, so we've also selected a couple of simple *braai* recipes to try. Whether the recipes in the book will work as well back home, away from the sunshine of the 'mother city', is open to question, but many of the ingredients are available in ethnic food shops, and an accompanying South African wine will undoubtedly help!

And good news for anyone suffering food intolerances: all of the recipes can be **gluten- and dairy-free** (see page 136).

SOUTH AFRICAN FOOD

With its 'rainbow cuisine', Cape Town offers diverse international food. However, we suggest trying restaurants that offer a modern 'take' on menus from the many indigenous cultures of South Africa (as all our recommended restaurants do).

Many native African dishes are high in carbohydrates, using **maize** kernels, dried and broken to make *samp*, or ground into a fine-grained porridge called *mieliepap*. Probably unappetising in quantity, these now make interesting accompaniments in innovative, contemporary dishes.

Meat from subsistence hunting was tough and unreliable, so needed to be slow-cooked in *potjie* (cast-iron pots). Delicious modern versions use tender venison (usually now ranched sustainably). Salted, spicy, **dried meats**, called *biltongs*, are a local favourite to chew as a quick snack. For the *braai*, traditional fare includes *boerewors* (farmers' sausage) and *sosaties* (spiced meat kebabs; recipe page 89).

The Cape Malay influence shows in *bobotie,* a rich mince dish with almonds, fruit chutney, spices and egg-based topping, and in delicious spicy stews called *bredies* (one Cape favourite, called 'Waterblommetjie Bredie', features the stems of water-lilies!

Fish and **shellfish** also feature strongly on menus (see page 43).

South African wines

Since apartheid times, when bulk South African wines were marketed under Bulgarian labels, a wine renaissance has begun.

White wine production is shifting from Chardonnay to the more sophisticated Sauvignon and Chenin Blanc. Rich and fruity blends of Merlot and Shiraz lead the reds, but the most truly South African red is Pinotage, a varietal hybrid between Pinot Noir and Hermitage, with a full, rich bouquet.

Stellenbosch produces the best reds, but excellent wines also come from Darling, Robertson, Paarl and Constantia, just outside Cape Town.

Don't be seduced by higher prices: cheaper brands, like Two Oceans and Porcupine Ridge, widely available in supermarkets and restaurants, are eminently drinkable. Look also for brands with the 'biodiversity and wine initiative' logo; these are from vineyards managed to protect native *fynbos*.

Constantia Uitsig vineyard

9

Fresh **fruit** is abundantly available, and makes excellent desserts, whether prepared in syrup or drenched in spicy wine sauces (see page 73).

PLANNING YOUR VISIT
When to go

We'd recommend visiting Cape Town in spring or autumn, when both weather and prices are moderate. In autumn (March-April), there's a mellowness to the landscapes and the weather is particularly benign, with temperatures rising to 25°C and rarely dropping below 15°C, low rainfall and mostly gentle winds. In spring (September-October) everything is fresh; the flowers are wonderful and the air is clear, but the weather is a little less reliable. Most days are bright and warm, but there can be strong south-easterly winds — called the 'Cape doctor'. These clear away the city smog, but can make walking uncomfortable, and they often bring the 'tablecloth' (the layer of

Fire is a natural phenomenon that helps sustain the native *fynbos* vegetation, but it can be hugely damaging too, so take care not to start fires. In winter 2005-06, there were major fires on Table Mountain and Lion's Head; one of these led to criminal proceedings against a British tourist who may have started the fire by discarding a cigarette. We checked that all our walks were still accessible, but some landmarks might change after the fire, and there might be minor alterations as paths are repaired.

cloud that blankets Table Mountain and sweeps down into the City Bowl; see photograph on page 4).

From November to March, temperatures are high but tolerable. There's very little rain but some risk of wild fires, and the 'tablecloth' can drape the mountain for days on end. This is holiday time locally: everywhere is busy, and prices are generally higher. From June to August, you can get excellent holiday deals, but the winter weather is more variable; really nice sunny days are interspersed with gloomy ones and heavy showers. Whenever you visit, remember that the 'tablecloth' is a regular feature of Cape Town that you should accept and appreciate (but if it's missing, get up Table Mountain at the first available opportunity!).

Where to stay

There is a huge choice of accommodation in Cape Town, from high-end chain hotels to budget hotels and self-catering apartments. As to location: the Sea Point, Waterfront and City Bowl areas are generally more expensive and less convenient for our walks. The Gardens area is better situated, and you can easily walk from there onto Table Mountain or the Lion's Head. There are some nice, convenient guest houses on Kloof Nek Road itself, the access route to both these walking areas, and various apartment complexes around Gardens.

We'd also recommend allowing time in your itinerary to stay a night or two around Hout Bay, Fish Hoek or Simon's Town, to enjoy the walks there more easily. Cape Town Tourism (see page 18) can provide information and book for you.

What to take

You won't need to take formal clothes: 'smart casual' is the norm in all but the most expensive Cape Town restaurants. You might need a **light jacket** or **windproof** to wear in the evenings. Toiletries, suncream and other essentials are no more expensive in Cape Town than at home, so save luggage searches and buy them locally. **Walking boots**, with good ankle support, are essential for some of our walks, and advisable for most of them, but trainers are okay for the gentler walks. Remember **thick socks** to go with the boots, and a **rucksack**. See also the section below on 'Planning your walks' for advice on outdoor clothing.

Medical advice

In health terms, the Cape Town area is one of the safest areas in Africa. Currently no special vaccinations are required, but you should check with your doctor before you travel (or see the UK Foreign & Commonwealth Office website at www.fco.gov.uk/travel). Malaria and bilharzia are mainly confined to the eastern half of South Africa, and you will only need malaria tablets if you plan to travel there.

The only significant health risk that walkers should be aware of is **African tick bite fever**. This is a *relatively* mild disease, compared to the diseases carried by ticks in Europe, and the precautions are exactly the same, but it can spoil your holiday if you are not aware of its effects! It's a bacterial infection spread by cattle ticks, and is found in rural areas where cattle or game animals (including larger antelope) gather: note that this can include Cape Point, for example. It occurs at any time of year, but particularly in spring, and incubation takes five to seven days after being bitten. The 'classic' symptom is reddish or black lesions where the bites occurred. The sufferer becomes very tired, with aches and pains, headaches, swollen glands and perhaps a fever. It is easily treated with a strong antibiotic, but you should consult a doctor if any of these symptoms appear.

The best advice, when walking in game areas, is to wear long trousers, tucked into your socks and use insect repellent.

Otherwise, there are very few dangerous wild animals in this area, although wild **baboons** should be treated with respect.

Watch out, too, for the **blister bush** (see right).

Probably the biggest risk for walkers is from the sun, heat and dehydration. Tap water in Cape Town and most surrounding areas is safe to drink. Water from *fast-running*

Blister bush

Although there are plenty of snakes in the Cape, they are generally more scared of humans than we are of them, so you can count yourself lucky if you spot one. Much more pain is caused to walkers by an innocuous-looking shrubby plant with celery-like leaves that produces yellow 'umbrellas' of flowers in early summer. It is aptly named the **blister bush** (*Peucedanum galbanum*). Avoid brushing heavily against this plant: any sap that gets onto your skin will react with sunlight to cause painful blisters. If you do get sap on you, cover the affected area immediately to keep out sunlight, and seek medical help if any blistering erupts.

13

streams is also generally safe to drink, although you should never drink water downstream from any habitation. Travellers should also remember the high prevalence of HIV/AIDS in Africa.

GETTING THE MOST FROM YOUR VISIT
Safety in Cape Town

The disparity between wealth and poverty in Cape Town means that some crime is inevitable, and many of the better-off locals live behind high security fences. Frankly, we've felt no more threatened in Cape Town than in, say, London, Paris or any large city. However, you should be aware of crime levels and take sensible precautions. Never leave property unattended, and keep valuables in a strongbox in the hotel or apartment. Carry a certified copy of your passport with you, rather than the document itself.

It's unwise to walk alone and some of the poorer areas are best avoided. Always keep to the busier, well-lit streets at night. Don't flaunt cameras, binoculars and expensive handbags. Keep your wallet or purse safe from pickpockets, and, as security against robbery, keep small change in your wallet or purse, and bank notes and credit cards hidden in an inside pocket.

Note also that in 2006 there was a spate of unpleasant muggings at various points on the Contour Path round Table Mountain. This popular route is *not* one of our walks, but a couple of our routes cross it or join it briefly. Security patrols have been greatly stepped up there since, but the best security

Leafy Greenmarket Square (Walk 1)

is to walk there in a group and certainly not alone. Busy weekends might be safer too.

Other safety precautions are simply common sense. Some of the walks are rough going, so don't tackle them alone. Mobile phones provide a useful safety precaution and work well in most areas (but keep them well hidden). Swim only in areas that have been marked as safe by lifeguards.

Getting around Cape Town

One area that caused us pause for thought in compiling this book was the safety of public transport. The better-off (mostly white) Capetonians tend to drive everywhere. That means the local 'Golden Arrow' buses are used mostly by the poorer (primarily black) community. Robberies do happen on these buses, but, much more likely, you will simply feel conspicuous and uncomfortable as a tourist on a predominantly work-person's bus. The local guidance is not to use these buses.

Until recently, the local trains were similar, but **Metrorail** has made a big effort to improve its reputation, with more police travelling on the trains. The coastal route down to Simon's Town has a good safety record, although we recommend travelling first class (called **MetroPlus**), and selecting a train carrying the Biggsy Restaurant Car, which provides extra safety – and meals or snacks (see Excursion 2).

The '**City Sightseeing**' buses are a boon. The 'red route' double-decker bus takes you around the main tourist haunts in the city and is a convenient way to get to Table Mountain. The 'blue route' takes you well out of the city, on a round trip to Kirstenbosch, Hout Bay and Camps Bay (see Excursion 1). All-day tickets for either route costs R100, and can be good value if you hop-on, hop-off several times.

We do *not* recommend the minibus taxis that locals use, although these will often tout for your business if you are walking in the city. However '**Rikki' taxis** are quite different and approved by the local Tourism Bureau. These mini-vans

have widely varying liveries, but always have square yellow stickers on the door. You can flag them down, but it is best to phone for one when you are ready to set off (☎ 021 423 4888). Be warned that they may take 20 minutes to arrive, and their routes are circuitous as they drop off and pick up other passengers. They are not

The City Sightseeing buses are a good way to see Cape Town and outlying areas, and of course there's always the cableway to whisk you up the mountain...

17

available on evenings or Sundays. The 'Rikki' service from Simon's Town railway station to Cape Point is also recommended (see Walk 12).

More orthodox taxis are not hugely expensive, with fares around R10 per kilometre, and tips are not generally expected. Note that it is not usual practice to hail a taxi on the street in Cape Town, but there are taxi ranks at the railway station, at the top of Adderley Street and at the Waterfront.

If you have a car, lock valuables in the boot, or, better still, leave them in your accommodation or carry them with you. In most car parks you will find a 'car guard' on duty, usually in some form of florescent vest. Sometimes these are appointed by the local community, but often they are self-appointed entrepreneurs. They do offer a genuine security service. It's worth having a chat with them before you set off, so they know you, and remember to tip them on your return if the car is safe (the going rate is one rand for each hour you were away).

Tourist information

We recommend a visit to Cape Town Tourism, at the corner of Castle and Burg Streets, early in your stay — it's included in our city walk (page 24). It offers information about places to visit, sells books, maps and postcards (and even snacks and internet access), and the staff are friendly and helpful.

If you want to do 'touristy things' to supplement our walks, you might want to buy the **Cape Town Pass** while you're there, with prices ranging from R275 for one day to R750 for six days. It's worth considering before our city walk, because the pass

The Tourist Office on Burg Street is a mine of information.

includes free admission to the castle and museums en route. It also gives free admission to Kirstenbosch Botanical Gardens, the aquarium, and World of Birds (see page 77), free 'City Sightseeing' bus tours, vouchers for Rikki taxis, and even a free township dinner (and much else). See www.thecapetownpass. co.za or (021 886 7080 for details.

Planning your walks

All our walks are accessible by **public transport**, using the bus or train links recommended (make sure you allow time to get the last transport back, or be prepared to phone for a 'Rikki' or a taxi). The timings are based on a steady but gentle walking pace, with occasional stops to admire the landscape, but you should allow extra time if you stop for a break, a picnic or a meal, or to botanise and birdwatch. Fit, single-minded walkers might complete the walks in half the time we suggest, and if you want more challenging exercise, the walks on Table Mountain can be combined in various permutations, as the text suggests.

The **fact box** for each walk recommends what **footwear and kit** to take. In general, we recommend carrying several layers of light clothes, including a long-sleeved shirt, to add or remove as needed, together with waterproofs, a first aid kit, whistle, compass, mobile phone, torch and spare socks and bootlaces. A sunhat, high-protection suncream and good insect repellent are essential, and make sure you have both shorts and long trousers. Always carry plenty of water (as a guide, decide what you normally drink, then double it), and some 'emergency food'.

Shopping for self-catering

Cape Town is a modern city and the nearest supermarket is never far away. The quality of the fruit, vegetables, meat and fish is generally high, and the prices significantly lower than at home. Familiar brands from home may well be available in the bigger supermarkets, but at a premium, so try the local equivalents instead. Casual sellers on Adderley Street near Golden Acre sell fruit and vegetables at good prices.

Check out your apartment when you arrive. Apartments generally have the basics, but utensils like vegetable peelers, whisks and corkscrews are sometimes missing. Supermarkets, like the Pick'n'Pay, ShopRite and 7 Eleven chains, can supply all these necessities and offer good quality food. Woolworths (not

Fynbos Deli at Kirstenbosch (left), flower seller in the Gardens district (below), and market stall on Adderley Street (bottom)

part of the UK chain) is slightly more expensive and upmarket, but has excellent vegetables and fruit and a good selection of wines.

For a big shopping trip, we recommend the Gardens Centre (℡ 021 418 4300) on Mill Street. The shopping mall here has an excellent Pick'n' Pay, as well as a Woolworths, pharmacy, health food, kitchenware and book shops, delis, banks, an internet café, and several nice coffee shops.

Everything here shuts fairly early (around 6-7pm), but there's a late-night Woolworths adjoining the petrol station situated almost

Pick'n'Pay has some ready-made hot meals available over the counter, like these ostrich burgers and chips with salsa — the burgers are delicious.

opposite Gardens Centre on Mill Street. Note that you pay for carrier bags in South Africa, so take your rucksack. The area around Kloof Street is also worth exploring for delis and wholefood shops.

Finding out more

If you want to explore the Cape Peninsula beyond what this small guide can offer, the series of five Table Mountain National Park maps by Peter Slingsby (Table Mountain, Hout Bay, Silvermine, Simon's Town, Cape Point) are essential and widely available. They are truly works of art and contain far more information than the walking maps in this book.

For more walks, we recommend two guides by local hiking guru, Mike Lundy: *Easy Walks in the Cape Peninsula* (Human & Rousseau) and *Best Walks in the Cape Peninsula* (Struik Publishers).

The most useful all-round guide to the wildlife and landscapes of the area is *Mountains in the Sea* (South African National Parks).

The authors

Michael and Sue Scott discovered Cape Town almost by accident, when marine biologist Sue was sailing from Cape Town Harbour to the remote island of Tristan da Cunha. On their first brief visit, they were inspired by

The authors at Marimba (see page 58)

the variety of wild flowers and wildlife they saw so easily from a city centre base, even without a hired car. The excellent restaurants they discovered on their walks were an added bonus! They have returned regularly since to explore the area more thoroughly, with self-catering cottages in Fish Hoek and Simon's Town providing bases to investigate walks in the Cape Peninsula. They pestered local friends and colleagues for advice on the best walks and places to eat — and for favourite local recipes to include in this book. Sue has done all the recipes — Michael is the sampler-in-chief!

Acknowledgements

For their help and guidance in preparing this book, Michael and Sue would like to thank Mike Lundy, Claus Tworeck of City Sightseeing, Brent Best (for the photograph on page 10), and the restaurant chefs and friends who kindly volunteered recipes for the book.

This city centre walk gives a flavour of the history, cultural diversity and lifestyles of Cape Town. If a full day walk is too demanding in the heat, you could do it in shorter sections. Since it's a circuit, the tour can begin wherever is most convenient for your base; use the plan inside the front cover to join where you like.

cape town highlights

WALK

The Castle of Good Hope makes a good **starting point**, and the red route City Sight-seeing bus stops outside. There's lots to see on this walk, but the choice is so much a matter of personal taste, we haven't attempted timings. If you have dead-lines, use the plan on the inside front cover to help you complete the circuit in time. *(Note that, as in common usage in Cape Town, we omit 'Street' etc from street names.)*

The massive, five-sided **Castle of Good Hope** was completed in 1679, making it South Africa's oldest occupied building. It has never seen action, but remains the headquarters for the Western Cape military command. There's been lots of restora-tion, including the original moat and wooden bridge. The governor's residence inside has some fine Cape Dutch

See plan inside front cover.

Distance: about 6.5 km (4 mi); allow anything from 4 to 8h, depending on how often you stop.

Grade: Easy walking, but can be hot and tiring; little shade.

Equipment: 'sensible' shoes, sunhat, money for shopping and refreshments

Transport: 🚌 red City Sightseeing bus or taxi to the Castle of Good Hope (or 🚗: park in the secure, pay-on-exit car park on Grand Parade opposite the castle).

Refreshments on route: plenti-ful and frequent!

Points of interest:

Castle of Good Hope: 09.30-16.00 daily; admission R20 (Sundays R10)

District Six Museum: 09.00-16.00 (15.00 Mon); closed Sun. Admission by donation (R10 usual)

Iziko South African Museum: 10.00-17.00 daily; admission R10

Planetarium, adjacent to Iziko Museum: shows at 14.00 Mon-Fri; noon, 13.00 and 14.30 Sat/Sun; admission R20

Bo-Kaap Museum: 09.30-16.30; closed Sunday and holidays; admission R5

Koopmans-de Wet House: 09.30-16.00 *Tue-Thu only*; admission R5

25

Governor's residence at the castle

furniture and paintings from the celebrated William Fehr collection. The Dolphin Pool in the far right corner was an indulgence of the first governor, Willem van der Stel, restored in 1982 as a pleasantly cool corner. There are guided walks round the castle, leaving at 11.00, 12.00 and 14.00 Mon-Sat, or map leaflets (R10) offer self-guided tours. Inside the entrance on the left, the De Goewerneur Café serves refreshments and meals.

Coming out of the castle, **Grand Parade** in front of you is where colonial troops once mustered, but today it's a car park and open air market. Turn left onto Buitenkant, and walk up three blocks to Albertus. On the far corner is the **District 6 Museum** (1), a moving reminder of South Africa's less than glorious recent history. District 6, east of here, was home to around 55,000 mostly coloured people until 1966 when it was declared a 'white' area, and its inhabitants were removed to bleak townships on the Cape Flats. The suburb was demolished but never rebuilt, although in 2000 President Mbeki formally handed the confiscated land back to its original inhabitants, and work has begun to redevelop the area.

The displays in the District 6 Museum are a vivid record of the city's shameful past and more hopeful future, told with personal recollections and reconstructions.

Leaving the museum, retrace your steps down Buitenkant, then take the second left onto Darling, before Grand Parade. On the left, the former **City Hall** (2), built of granite and marble in 1905, is Cape Town's grandest public building, with a clock tower modelled on London's Big Ben but half the size (see photograph overleaf). It was from the balcony here that Nelson Mandela addressed a quarter-million throng shortly after his release from Robben Island prison in 1990.

Continue along Darling for another three blocks to Adderley. Turn right, past the impressive porticos of a bank, and you will come to the **Golden Acre flower market** (3), where vendors sell carnations, irises and proteas at reasonable prices. Retrace your steps to Darling, cross the road, and

The old City Hall

follow the narrow lane of Shortmarket, directly opposite. Two blocks on, you'll find yourself in cobbled **Greenmarket Square** (4), the bustling heart of the commercial area, originally built as a farmer's market. Today it hosts a plethora of intriguing stalls (don't be afraid to barter). Turning left, at the far end of the square is the **Old Town House** (5), dating from 1761 and now a museum and art gallery. Keep left along Longmarket, then turn right onto Adderley again.

As you walk up Adderley, on the left you'll see the **Groote Kerk** ('Great Church'; 6), the mother church of the Dutch Reformed (Calvinist) religion. Crossing Bureau, the next building on the left is the old **Slave Lodge** (7), which once housed up to 1000 slaves awaiting sale. It later became in succession: a brothel, a jail, a mental asylum, and the Cape Supreme Court. It now houses the Cultural History Museum.

As the road bends round to the right, the impressive building on your left is the **Houses of Parliament** (8; tours by appointment only), where, since 1994, multiracial democracy has flourished in a way that seemed impossible just a few years before. Following the road round, we reach **St George's Cathedral** (9), home church in Cape Town for the Anglican faith, designed by Herbert Baker in 1897.

Now return to Government Avenue — the leafy walkway between the parliament and the cathedral. This often hosts impromptu music and crafts stalls. Walk up it a short way, then bear right into **Company Gardens** (10), for much-needed shade beneath some magnificent trees. Only six hectares is left of what was once a vegetable garden three times that size, from which

Government Avenue hosts impromtu displays of music and dancing; in Company Gardens (right) the colonnaded Delville Wood Memorial commemorates the South African Soldiers who died in the First World War.

Jan van Riebeeck provisioned his Dutch East India Company ships in the late 17th century. In the middle of the garden, look for the statue to Cecil John Rhodes, the empire builder (1853-1902). There's a shady restaurant on the right here beneath the trees.

Continuing on the main track, look on the left for the statue of General Jan Smuts (1870-1950; photograph page 70), the mountaineer and conservationist, whose favourite route up Table Mountain we follow in Walk 6. At the top end of the gardens is a grandiose, colonnaded **memorial** (11) honouring South African soldiers who fell during World War I. In front of you is the **Iziko South African Museum** (12), which has excellent natural history and geological collections, with the adjacent **Planetarium** (13; allow at least two hours for a visit). Otherwise, turn right at the memorial, out of the gates, and go left along Queen Victoria Street, passing the Planetarium, with its copper dome. The City Sightseeing bus stops here, if you've had enough for one day.

Follow the pavement round to the right, passing the **Jumu'a Mosque** (14) of Cape Town and a filling station, then turn right into Long Street. Note the **Turkish Baths** (15), which date from 1908 but have been restored and are still very popular. Continue down **Long Street**, a veritable Aladdin's Cave of a thorough-fare. There are bookshops galore, and restaurants of every

ethnic origin, including African — Mama Africa (see page 34) is highly recommended. Several buildings have Victorian facades of real charm, even if some seem frozen in a different era, like the Overseas Visitors Club UK.

Continuing down Long Street, just as its charm gives way to soulless modernism, turn left onto Waal/Wale, and follow the hill up three featureless blocks, crossing the broad boulevard of Buitengracht. The houses now become brightly coloured as you enter the Malay Quarter, known as **Bo-Kaap**. This district is changing fast, with houses selling for inflated prices, and the character is beginning to drain from the area. However, the **Bo-Kaap Museum** (16) on the left at number 71 seeks to preserve all that. The displays inside are being remodelled, but, when we visited, one room featured a thought-provoking display of the challenges faced by modern Muslim women, while another focussed on the workers who built Cape Town. The Community Centre upstairs has wonderful photos of life in this vibrant part of Cape Town culture.

Colourful houses at Bo-Kaap

Exiting the museum, double back to Buitengracht, turn left and continue along for around five blocks until you reach Strand. As you turn right here, notice the **Lutheran Church** (17) on the opposite corner. When this was built in 1771, it was designed to pass as a warehouse, because only the Dutch Reformed faith was recognised by the authorities, but it was subsequently redesigned to be more church-like. Next door, Martin Melck House is a fine 18th-century Cape Dutch townhouse, which now houses the **Gold of Africa Museum**.

Continue down Strand, crossing Long Street, and just beyond on the right, dwarfed by tower blocks behind, is **Koopmans-de Wet House** (18), a museum dedicated to a more elegant, but very much less egalitarian, age. It's a classic 18th-century Cape house, where Marie Koopmans-de Wet lived with her sixteen children. She was a socialite, patron of the arts and Afrikaner nationalist. She clearly had a taste for fine living, but the museum notes the singular absence of paintings of the many servants who made that life possible!

A short way beyond, turn right into Burg, and the **Tourist Information Office** (19) is on the right. This is full of information, with helpful staff and an internet cafe. Both red and blue City Sightseeing buses stop directly opposite, so this makes an excellent point to end the tour.

If you left a car at Grand Parade, continue along Strand. Beside the **Golden Acre Centre**, descend into an underpass and find the railway station exit. Walk past the **railway station** (itself a fine building dating from 1875), cross over to Buiten-kant and walk back to the castle, with the car park opposite.

Mama Africa

The quality of city centre restaurants in Cape Town is generally pretty high. Mama Africa stood out for us, though, with its zany exterior on Long Street, and its interior is just as much fun. Although it's young-at-heart, it welcomes all age groups, locals and visitors alike.

Starters range from vegetable samosas to crocodile in satay sauce. **Mains** include curries and *bobotie*, as well as seasonal stuffed venison and wild game mixed grill. There's a good **seafood** range too, and several **vegetarian** options. The charming and helpful staff were fully clued up about gluten- and dairy-free eating. Live music starts mid-evening (R10 cover charge added), but is great fun if you're in the mood. They're also open lunchtimes from Tuesday to Friday, which fits nicely with our city centre walk (Walk 1).

Mama Africa — the fun interior and (right) their 'Dovi Zimbabwean' (a chicken, peanut and spinach stew)

MAMA AFRICA
178 Long Street, Cape Town
(021 424 8634
mama@maweb.co.za
Mon-Sat 19.00 till late; also Tue-Fri
   from 11.00-16.00; closed Sun
RRR   (CC: V, MC, AM, DC)

restaurants

eat

Bobotie

Bobotie, a tasty Malay dish, normally includes slices of bread and buttermilk, but this gf, df version just leaves them out. If one of you doesn't eat eggs either, split the meat mixture into two portions before cooking and leave the egg topping off one of them; it doesn't look quite so attractive as the traditional bright yellow version, but is still delicious.

Pre-heat the oven to 180°C. Fry the onions and mince in oil until browned. Add raisins, apricots, apple, almonds, jam, curry powder, lemon juice and seasoning to taste. Turn into a baking dish and spread evenly. Tuck bay leaves into the mixture and bake uncovered 30 min.

Beat the eggs with the turmeric, a little milk and seasoning, and pour over the meat mixture. Return to oven for 10 min —or until set. Serve with plain rice and perhaps a green vegetable or a *sambal* (see page 137).

<u>Ingredients (for 2 people)</u>
1 onion, sliced
500 g lamb or beef mince
Oil for frying
1/4 cup raisins
1/4 cup chopped dried
  apricots
1 apple, peeled and grated
1/4 cup toasted flaked
  almonds
2 tbsp apricot jam
1 tsp medium curry powder
2 tbsp lemon juice
6 lemon or bay leaves
2 eggs
milk
1/4 tsp turmeric
Salt & black pepper

recipes

eat

This is an ideal 'shakedown' walk to get acclimatised to walking the Cape, and to introduce the *fynbos* habitat. It's mostly flat and easy, with spectacular scenery. It follows the route of a water pipe, although the walk varies from a wide jeep track to a rough footpath.

pipe track

WALK

Kloof Nek roundabout is a hub for attractive Cape Town walks. It's possible to walk up to here from town, but a bit of a slog. Better to drive, hire a taxi, or use the red City Sightseeing bus (you'll have to ask to be let off at the roundabout, but most drivers are cooperative).

The walk starts up a set of granite steps directly above the **Kloof Nek roundabout**, with dramatic views of the Lion's Head to your right. Within a few moments the **pipe** that gives this walk is name appears beneath some stone pines. It was built in the late 19th century to carry water from the 'Back Table' of Table Mountain (see Walk 7)

Distance: about 10 km (6 mi) there and back; around 4h

Grade: easy, but rough underfoot in places; minimal ascent; some shade

Risk of vertigo: minor; at the end of the walk only

Equipment: stout walking shoes, sunhat, suncream, warm clothing and wind- and waterproofs, water

Transport: 🚌 red City Sightseeing bus or taxi to the Kloof Nek roundabout; 🚗 if driving, take the turning off the Kloof Nek roundabout signed to the cableway and park immediately on left (note car park closes at 19.00).

Refreshments: none en route, but see page 42 for one possibility for a meal at the end of the walk.

Points of interest:
Views to Twelve Apostles above
Views to Camp Bay and Bakoven below
Typical *fynbos* vegetation

into a reservoir above the city, via the Woodhead Tunnel and down Slangolie Ravine (where this walk ends). The engineering is impressive, as you will see in places. The path gets slightly rough, as you duck under the pipe (**7min**) and have to pick your way over tree roots. Just beyond this, a wooden bridge was burnt out by a fire in 2006, necessitating a bit of a gully scramble. Hopefully it will soon be repaired.

Pass below the rather grandiose water filtration plant on the left, and drop down a steep flight of steps into **Diepsloot Gorge (15min)**. The path beyond zigzags upwards — take comfort from the fact that this is the steepest stretch on the entire walk! Now the path levels off, between beautiful banks of Proteas. As the path sweeps round another gully **(25min)**, **Tommy's Aqueduct** carries the pipe across the gorge to your right.

A long, easy and very flowery stretch of path now follows, until you plunge into the shade of a scrub hedge, and the path becomes a little rough. You'll pass a large sign for Blinkwater Ravine, then a bit further on, a sign on the left pointing up to the **Diagonal Path (45min)**. Ignore

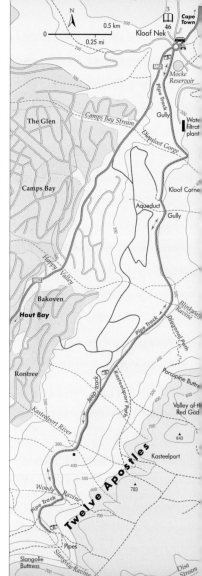

At the junction with the signpost up to Kasteelsport

that and keep on the contouring path signed towards Kasteels-port.

Soon another waymarker points uphill towards **Kasteels-port (1h)**. Again ignore this siren call, and keep on the flat, signed to Slangolie. A short way further on, you might spot a bench on a rocky knoll to the right; it offers spectacular views over Camps Bay and makes a satisfying point to turn around if you've had enough. Continuing on, beyond another bushy

Note this spot; the footpath for the return leaves the jeep track to the right here.

stretch, the path meets an old jeep track, zigzagging up from below *(note this junction carefully for the way back!)*. The walking now is easy, until the jeep track ends at a broad **turning point (1h15min)** beneath another ravine.

The onward path is obvious, passing a fine stone building with an arched roof. When a rusty waymarker post, half hidden in the trees, points up to **Woody Ravine (1h30min)**, keep on the

Fire heath is a flower that flourishes after fires on the hillside. Below right: Slangolie Ravine

main path, which soon rises quite steeply onto a narrow ledge blasted below the cliff, with the pipeline still evident here and there. Round the corner, the path meets an impressive set of stone steps. Climb these to a **stone platform beside the pipe** (**1h45min**), for an impressive view to the rocky scree of **Slangolie Ravine**. We

recommend this as an appropriate point to rest, before turning back — the scrambly path beyond soon becomes steep and dangerous.

Retrace your steps back to the **Kloof Nek roundabout** (**4h**), admiring the magnificent views. Be careful to pick up the path where it branches right off the descending jeep track, or you will end up in Camps Bay with a long walk back to Cape Town!

Café Paradiso

The food in Eugene and Deon Labuschagne's restaurant is delicious, and the atmosphere pleasantly informal. We've walked in straight off Table Mountain, hot and dusty, and been served dinner without hesitation (you could sit on the outside patio if you feel too dishevelled).

The Mediterranean-themed menu changes with season, but we'd rave about the lamb **soup**, warm goats' cheese **salad**, lamb shank balsamico and ostrich *bobotie* (this contains flour and cream, but the staff are informed and helpful on dietary requirements). The **meze** as a **starter** or **main course** caters for all diets, and there is an excellent range of **wines**, available by the glass.

Café Paradiso — and their warm beetroot salad

A 'business' lunch costs R75, and there's even a loyalty card to tempt you back. To get here from Table Mountain or Lion's Head, walk down Kloof Nek, turn right down steep

CAFÉ PARADISO
110 Kloof Street, Cape Town
(021 423 8653
www.cafeparadiso.co.za
cafep@intekom.co.za
daily from 09.30-23.00*
*opens 09.00 Sat/Sun, 12.00 Mon
RR   (CC: V, MC, AM, DC)

Bellevue Road, go left at the foot onto Kloof Street, and it's not far beyond, on the left.

restaurants

eat

Pickled fish

Eugene from Café Paradiso offered us this recipe, which is served cold as a starter or light lunch with a green salad. It's also a good way of using surplus fish from a fishing trip, or ready-cooked from the grill or *braai*.

Cut the fish into steaklets or chunks, dip in seasoned flour and fry in oil until golden brown and crispy. Fry the onion in oil until soft. Add all the other ingredients, bring to the boil, then remove from heat. Pour the hot sauce over the fish and let stand overnight.

Ingredients (for 2 people)
Firm fish
Flour for dusting
Oil for frying
1 large onion, sliced
1 tsp salt
1 bay leaf
2 tsp curry powder
1/2 tsp turmeric
1 tbsp sugar
2 peppercorns
1/3 cup white vinegar
1 cup water

We love to eat fish, but as Sue is a marine biologist, we are aware of the unseen destruction that indiscriminate fishing methods wreak in the sea, and we like to support fisheries that cause the least damage. It's often very difficult to find out which these are, but in South Africa you can get a credit-card sized guide produced by SASSI (Southern African Sustainable Seafood Initiative). Or download the guide before you travel (www.wwf. org.za/sassi) and then refer to it in markets and restaurants. Fortunately, snoek, yellowtail and bluefish (all popular on the Cape Peninsula and delicious) are on the 'green' (ok to eat) list, as are rock lobsters from the south and west (but not east!) coasts, squid (calamari), octopus and mussels.

recipes

eat

This lovely walk is only briefly demanding. As you wind clockwise around the Lion's Head, you're accompanied by abundant flowers and birdsong. Reaching the top is a satisfying achievement, and you're guaranteed the best views in Cape Town.

lion's head

WALK

This is a popular walk with Capetonians. It gets fairly strenuous near the top, when you will briefly need some agility and a head for heights, but is mostly easy walking on well-graded paths. (You can skip scaling the peak if you prefer, but you'll miss spectacular views.)

From the **Kloof Nek roundabout**, walk up Signal Hill Road, to the **signposted start of the walk** about 500m up on the left (opposite the parking area). Ascend the steep but easy gravel track. Wonderful views soon open out, over the City Bowl and harbour, and up to Table Mountain. Above you, a line of pine trees marks the final

Distance: 6 km (3.5 mi); 3h30min

Grade: mostly easy, but moderate rock scrambling on upper stretch; ascent of 380 m (1250 ft); minimal shade

Risk of vertigo: severe — but brief — near the top

Equipment: stout walking shoes essential (walking boots recommended), sunhat, suncream, warm clothing, wind- and waterproofs, water

Transport: 🚌 red City Sightseeing bus or taxi to the Kloof Nek roundabout; 🚗 if driving, turn right off the roundabout onto Signal Hill Road and park about 500 m up, in a small pull-in on the right beneath tall gum trees.

Refreshments: none en route, but see page 42 for a suggestion.

Points of interest:
Climb to 669 m (2195 ft) summit of Lion's Head
Spectacular views over Cape Town
Rare silver trees

route to the summit (these were badly burnt in a fire in 2006, and may not survive). Soon you enter an open forest of silver trees — this is one of three areas on Table Mountain which are the only natural home for this endangered species.

Not far up the track there is a **bench** on a corner (**10min**), with views of the cableway and Kloof Nek and, after a few

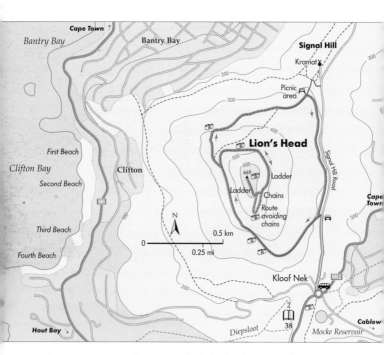

minutes more, another one which looks down on Camps Bay. Then **shallow steps (20min)** lead upwards to the rocky base of the Lion's Head. Coming out of the silver trees, the *fynbos* vegetation becomes more open and shrubby. This is a good place to pause and try to spot the many small birds singing from the bushes.

At a **signpost with three arrows (30min)**, carry straight on uphill. (But if you want to miss out the steep parts of the Lion's

Head and do an easy circular route instead, turn left downhill here, picking up the notes below from the 2h30min-point.) Shortly, you can look down on the 'Lion's Rump' — the long profile of Signal Hill ahead. After this the footpath becomes steeper, but never difficult. The sedimentary rock erodes naturally into convenient steps, and the difficult bits have been well built. At the sign that says 'down', continue *up!*

Now you come to a steel ladder, and, a little further on, a chain helps you across an exposed section. This is easy to negotiate, but prepares you for what's ahead. When you come to an **isolated stone pine tree** on your right (**50min**), a stone steps lead you towards a small cliff face with **two sets of vertical chains**. These are not all that tricky to negotiate with care (see photo), but you need both hands free, so stow cameras, binoculars etc before you start. However, if it looks too daunting, there's an easier alternative route, clearly signposted to the left. This continues along the contour, then winds upwards. It feels a bit exposed in places, but is easy if you are careful, and takes about 10 minutes longer than the vertical chain ascent.

Several tall pines now indicate that you're near the top. The last sections are no more difficult, but run along a ridge which

is narrow in places, so you do need a good head for heights. The path includes another metal ladder, and some of the rock steps are quite high. Not entirely reassuringly, there is barbed wire to catch you if you slip in some of the most dangerous places!

Eventually you reach the paved **summit of Lion's Head (1h30min)** with its amazing panoramic view, unobscured by obtrusive safety railings! Take time to savour these vistas ('tablecloth' permitting), then begin the return trip, initially by the same route.

Spring flowers below the Lion's Head

The chain-free route is not quite so easy to locate going down. To find it, go right when you're roughly level with the **third pine tree down**. (If you prefer, some people find the chains easier to descend than ascend.)

When you're back at the **signpost with three arrows (2h30min)**, turn right. Shortly after the junction, big outcrops of rounded rocks beside the path make a good spot to rest. The path, which leads down the lion's 'back', is steepish, and quite loose and eroded in places, so take care. At a post with no sign, where a small path heads right, follow the main path round to the left, and the incline becomes easier. Soon the path becomes wide and gravelled, and leads down to the *Kramat* (Muslim tomb) and a **picnic area** beside the road to Signal Hill. Just before you reach these, turn right on a small path that runs into the bushes, past two **cannons**. This path, often ablaze with colourful *Watsonia* flowers, now contours round the hillside, back to the start of the trail and **Kloof Nek (3h30min)**.

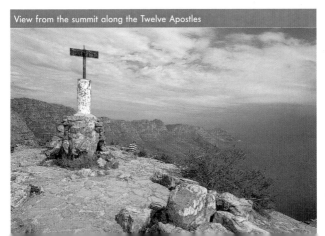

View from the summit along the Twelve Apostles

The Restaurant on Table Mountain

This may not be the best restaurant in this book, but it certainly has the best location, perched on the top of Table Mountain with spectacular views along the Twelve Apostles mountain range. It's well situated for Walks 2, 3, 4 (and 6 at a stretch), and the food is perfectly acceptable.

THE RESTAURANT ON TABLE MOUNTAIN
Near the top cableway station, Table Mountain, Cape Town
(021 424 8181
www.tablemountain.net
(no e-mail)
daily from 08.30 until half an hour before the last cable car
RR   (CC: V, MC, AM, DC)

They serve **breakfast** until 11.30, and you can buy cableway tickets inclusive of breakfast. **Lunch** and **light snacks** are served from 11.30.

The best value is to load a plate from the tempting **salad bar**, then add a side portion of chips. There's even a reasonable **wine** selection.

The restaurant closes half an hour before the last cable car, anytime from 17.30 in winter to 21.30 in high summer. Check with the cableway before setting off — but beware that the cableway and restaurant close earlier if the wind gets up. There are plans to expand the restaurant with an even larger outdoor terrace.

restaurants

eat

Butternut squash is a popular vegetable in South Africa, but we were distinctly unimpressed with it as a vegetable until we learned that you don't just boil it. It is delicious baked, as part of a stew, or even made into crisps and scattered on a salad. There's another recipe using this flexible vegetable on page 129.

Butternut squash salad

This is a delicious and colourful salad, great with a *braai*; you can make it in advance, adding the rocket just before serving.

Preheat the oven to 200°C. Peel the squash and remove the seeds. Cut into 2 cm cubes and toss in olive oil in an ovenproof dish, or place on foil in oven tray. Season lightly and sprinkle with rosemary (or use rosemary seasoning). Roast in oven about 35 min, until tender.

Allow to cool, then add to halved olives and tomatoes in a bowl large enough to toss gently with sprinkled lemon juice and perhaps a little more olive oil. Season to taste and serve on a bed of rocket leaves, with pumpkin seeds scattered over.

Ingredients (for 4 people)
1 butternut squash
olive oil
Rosemary, or rosemary seasoning
Salt & black pepper
Cherry or small plum tomatoes, halved
Black olives, de-stoned and halved
Lemon juice
Rocket leaves
Toasted pumpkin seeds (optional)

recipes

eat

This is a delightful, easy walk over the 'Table Top', just long enough that you don't need to feel guilty about using 'mechanical uplift' to carry you up and back down Table Mountain. The restaurant on top (see page 50) offers a nice bonus at the start or end of the walk.

maclear's beacon

WALK

The walk uses the easiest way onto Table Mountain — the cable car. It begins and ends at the upper cableway station, so get a return ticket unless you want to combine this walk with Walk 5 and descend Platteklip Gorge. The path over the top is a gentle and popular stroll, much used by locals and tourists alike. The return route is a little rougher underfoot with fantastic, vertiginous views, but you can retrace your steps along the easy route if you don't want to be too adventurous.

In fine weather, the scenery is glorious, but remember that the weather on Table Mountain is unpredictable. Up here, it can change from bakingly

Distance: 5.3km (3.5 mi); about 2h

Grade: easy, but the route back is rough in places; negligible ascents/descents

Risk of vertigo: minor to moderate on route back (can be avoided)

Equipment: stout walking shoes essential (walking boots *strongly recommended*), sunhat, suncream, warm clothing, wind- and waterproofs, water, money for cablecar and refreshments

Transport: 🚌 red City Sightseeing bus or taxi to the lower cableway station, then cable car to top station (R60 single, R120 return; check latest fares at www.tablemountain.net)

Refreshments: Table Mountain restaurant at start and end of the walk (see page 50)

Points of interest:
Dramatic views over Cape Town.
Maclear's Beacon
Memorial to General Jan Smuts

hot to decidedly chilly within a few hours, so be prepared for all weathers. Stick to the marked path in case the 'tablecloth' comes down, and **do not use the return clifftop route in windy, wet or misty conditions.** Before you set off, check when the last cable car down is scheduled. En route, listen for the siren that signals the cableway is closing because of severe weather. If you

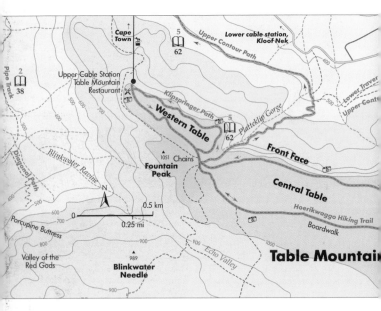

hear it, return to the upper cable station as quickly as you can, or you face a long walk down!

As you leave the top station, head towards the shop and restaurant (see page 50). Here you will want to pause to admire the view southwards along the Twelve Apostles, and look for dassies on the rocks. Note also the public conveniences! Then **start the walk:** make your way over a wooden viewing platform onto a well-built concrete tourists' path and follow this. Before long (**10min**), take the right fork signed for the **Klipspringer Path,** just before the 'Tapestry of Life' display board.

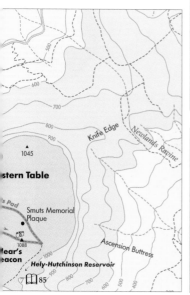

DASSIES

The dassie (properly called the rock hyrax) is a bizarre creature. It looks like a large guinea-pig, but is actually a close relative of the elephant (check out its hoof-like feet for a clue). Dassies often can be seen basking on the rocks on sunny days, both high on Table Mountain and around rocky coasts. They survive well on the tough vegetation up here, so resist the temptation to feed them. This only encourages them to scavenge — and they bite!

The path is now made of concrete and rock — easy walking. When the Klipspringer Path forks left (**15min**), keep straight ahead for Platteklip Gorge and Maclear's Beacon — as indicated by a low-lying plaque. Shortly after, you come to a steepish descent. Use the chains and posts to secure your way down the rocks. Soon you will see the top of Platteklip Gorge to your left *(Walk 5 joins here)*. Ignore this, and follow the broad path straight ahead, with painted yellow footprints that mark your route all the way to the beacon.

Where a sign on the right points to **Echo Valley** (**30min**),

Yellow-painted footprints mark the way to Maclear's Beacon (just visible in the background to the right), while frogs croak in the marshy *fynbos*.

keep slightly *left*, with nice views over the Hely-Hutchinson and Woodhead reservoirs (Walk 7) to your right. You join a **boardwalk (40min)** — listen for frogs croaking in springtime — and the rocky knoll of the beacon is visible ahead of you. Just before you make a brief ascent to the final plateau, you pass a fine stand of king proteas on your right. On the plateau, the yellow footprints are sometimes wayward, but the route is clear as you rise to the conspicuous pyramidal cairn of **Maclear's**

Beacon — the top of Table Mountain at 1088 m (**55min**). Pause here and enjoy the spectacular views.

If you want an easy stroll, retrace your steps. Otherwise, pick your way down the rocks beyond the cairn and join a path below that bends sharply back to the left, almost in the direction you came. Look for the 'Smuts Pad/Smuts Track' marker beside the path. Just beyond it, on a rock face to the left, is a plaque commemorating Jan Christiaan Smuts (1870-1950), a keen mountaineer, Boer war hero and South African Prime Minister who first called for measures to protect Table Mountain in 1923.

A well-made path now picks its way onward through the *fynbos*, with short stretches of boardwalk. When the path comes close to the precipitous edge of the '**Front Face**' (**1h15min**), follow the path *very* carefully, as it squeezes between rocks. You suddenly find yourself looking down into **Platteklip Gorge** (**1h25min**), and the path moves away from the edge. The path becomes a little indistinct, but soon veers sharply inland until you rejoin the main path, with a flurry of yellow footprints. Turn right and briefly retrace your steps. *(The route down Platteklip Gorge is signed just beyond this point if you want to make the steep descent this way; see Walk 5.)*

After you climb back up the post-and-chain section, look for a stony path that bends sharply back to the right up the hill. At the top of this slope, a sign confirms that you have rejoined a new stretch of the **Klipspringer Path** (**1h40min**). Follow this for an easy 20-minute walk back to the **top cableway station** (**2h**), keeping straight on wherever there's a fork to the left.

Marimba

This isn't a restaurant to visit straight off the hill, and it's a little off our city walk, but it's perfect for a nice evening out. Dress is 'smart casual', and the atmosphere is relaxed but sophisticated. It's described as 'sexy and seductive, with nightly live ambient dinner Afro jazz and no cover charge.' The Marimba team of chefs are rightly celebrated for their modern take on African cuisine.

The menu changes regularly, but typical **starters** include spiced calamari, and ostrich pâté with corn bread and gooseberry jam. As **mains**, we had a succulent ostrich fillet, and an *ndebele tagine*, an African dish of lamb, venison or seafood, slow-cooked in a clay pot (there's a helpful

MARIMBA
Corner of Heerengracht and Coen Steytler Ave, beneath Cape Town International Convention Centre (entrance 5); parking R10 for customers
(021 418 3366
www.marimbaSA.com
info@marimbaSA.com
Mon-Fri: 08.00-late; Sat: 18.00-late; closed Sun
RRR (CC: V, MC, AM, DC)

glossary in the menu to explain everything). **Sweets** are to die for, the **wine list** is excellent, and they claim a selection of 28 single malts to end a perfect meal! It's open for indulgent **breakfasts** on weekdays too.

restaurants

eat

Spiced ostrich fillet with prune-potato bake

This delicious recipe, adapted from one given us by Marimba, gets its special flavour from *dukka*, a nuts and spice mixture available in tins.

Pre-heat the oven to 180°C. In a saucepan, bring the prunes to the boil with 200 ml water and sugar, then take off the heat. Slice the potatoes thinly. Build up the bake in a greased oven dish: place the largest potato slices in a circle, top with a layer of seasoning and cheese. Use progressively smaller potato slices for the layers above. Include chopped prunes in the last two layers, and end with potatoes topped with cheese. Bake for about 30-40 min (test with a skewer).

Make the sauce: reduce the wine by half, add the beef stock and reduce until slightly thickened. Season to taste, whisk in a knob of butter (optional).

Coat both sides of the fillets with dukka, and season lightly. Heat a small pan, add a little oil and/or butter and seal the fillets each side. Place in the oven and roast 8 min, turning after 4 min. Remove and keep warm until the potato bake is ready. Then reheat the sauce, place a potato bake and an ostrich fillet on each plate, drizzle the sauce over fillet and serve as shown.

Ingredients (for 2 people)
2 ostrich fillets
20 g dried prunes
Sugar (to taste)
50 g grated cheese (or substitute 50 g lightly fried onions)
3 smallish potatoes, thinly sliced
2 handfuls rocket
200 ml beef stock
1 cup red wine
10 g *dukka*
Salt & black pepper

recipe

eat

Maybe this is the masochist's route up Table Mountain, with the effortless cableway so close, but you will treat 'the Table' with new respect once you've conquered its north face on this dramatic path which ascends to the Western Table via Platteklip Gorge!

platteklip gorge
WALK

To us, this seems the perfect way to *really* get to know Table Mountain: a demanding but well-built path to the summit, then a leisurely downward journey by cable car, rather than a joint-sapping descent on foot. (You can always retrace your steps on the way back if you prefer the exercise, taking around 5 hours for the round trip).

The Table Mountain National Park authorities have made fantastic progress in recent years upgrading the path, with gabions and massive boulder steps, and work is continuing. The footing is secure all the way, and it's really only the relentless 'up-ness' of the path that earns this walk a 'strenuous' grade.

Distance: about 4km (2.5 mi) on the map, but distance here irrelevant; allow up to 3h.

Grade: moderate-strenuous, especially in hot weather; ascent of 710 m (2330 ft); some shade in the gorge

Risk of vertigo: minor-moderate

Equipment: strong shoes essential (walking boots *strongly recommended*), sunhat, suncream, warm clothing, wind- and waterproofs, water, money for return cable car (currently R60 single; update at www. tablemountain.net) and refreshments; walking pole(s) helpful

Transport: 🚌 red City Sightseeing bus or taxi to the lower cableway station

Refreshments: Table Mountain Restaurant at the end of the walk; none en route and only one reliable stream, so take plenty to drink!

Points of interest:
Dramatic views over Cape Town
Nice proteas by the path
Impressive gorge scenery

Any moderately fit person will be able to complete it, but allow plenty of time and don't rush. You will need to watch your footing throughout the walk, so, if you want to admire the dramatic panoramas of Cape Town below or the cliffs above, stop at some secure vantage point — don't try to walk and look!

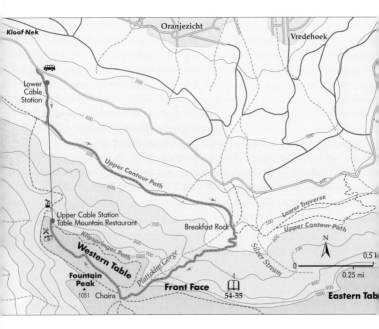

Before you set off, check that the cableway is running. En route, listen for the siren that signals the cableway is closing because of severe weather. If you hear it, be aware that the easy option down may well be denied you; consider whether you really want to continue on, knowing that you'll have to come back the same way as you've slogged up, and that the restaurant will be closed when you get to the top.

The walk starts at the bottom end of the bus park, just below the lower cableway station. You begin up a neat set of

National Park sign at the start of the walk

steps, passing a National Park sign, but the path quickly becomes rough and stony. The path climbs more or less directly and quite steeply beneath the wires of the cable car. When you reach a T-junction with the **Contour Path** (**20min**) round the side of the mountain, a warning sign advises against the route straight up the mountain (not that you'd be tempted!). Instead, follow the **signpost left towards Platteklip Gorge**. The path becomes fairly level, if rough in places. It winds round past some fine protea bushes and beneath dramatic blocky cliffs. A **finger post** (**30min**) alerts you to the fact that the gorge is 25 minutes ahead, but you may be quicker than this estimate! When the path forks (**40min**), keep right. Five minutes later you cross a **stream** (**45min**): it is safe to drink, and the last reliable water you will pass, so take the chance to fill your water bottle.

Shortly after this, you will meet a well-constructed path coming up from below. Platteklip Gorge now towers above you — '*platte klip*' means 'flat rock', and you may ponder where this name might have come from! You now make your way up some well-built boulder steps, held in place by stone-filled, wire gabion baskets. Soon you come to another signboard pointing

up into **Platteklip Gorge** (**50min**). The nick in the rocks high above is your objective, and the only way now is on and upwards.

The timing from here on up is a matter of personal taste: some keep-fit enthusiasts head up at a steady jog, but we tend to find a nice flower or view to photograph every ten minutes or so, as a good excuse for a breather! The path zig-zags unremittingly up the hill. Occasionally it runs along the contour for fifty metres or so as a welcome respite, but mostly it climbs steadily. The footing is mostly secure (it can be

The 'wondrous steep' walls of Platteklip Gorge

slippery in wet weather), although some of the steps are large. As a rough guide, we suggest allowing around 1h30min for the ascent. Do stay on the path: it really is the best way to go, and shortcuts cause erosion that makes the walk worse for those who follow.

Gradually the nick in the rock comes closer, and you find yourself wedged between two massive bluffs — in 1634, Peter Mundy described this section as 'wondrous steep, the rocks on each side like monstrous walls'. The path here is neatly stepped, and you may now find cooling wind whipping down from above. Finally you emerge in a low valley on the **summit plateau** (**Western Table; 2-3h**). *(You meet Walk 4 here; if you wish, turn left and follow it to Maclear's Beacon and back, adding about 1h30min.)*

Turn right for Table Mountain restaurant and the easy route home (Walk 4 gives full details). A small rock face is your final challenge, but there are poles and chains to haul yourself up. Then the path becomes an easy concrete and rock highway. Keep to paths along the left (south) side of the plateau, and you will soon see the chimney of the shop and welcoming restaurant. It will take you about 10 minutes' walking to get there, but stop and read the interpretative plaques and admire the view from the various lookouts. It's only five minutes from the restaurant to the upper cableway station — and then just four minutes to descend by cable car what you have just taken two-three hours to ascend (but without the same sense of achievement!).

This classic Table Mountain walk is demanding but satisfying. It follows the 'Smuts Track' through the welcome shade of forest to the summit plateau, then descends down the valley shown on the cover of the book, full of king proteas.

skeleton gorge and nursery ravine

WALK

The walk starts at the upper parking area at **Kirstenbosch Gardens** (where the bus also stops). Pay to enter (currently R27) and, once inside, head for the tearoom (it does great breakfasts). Climb the small steps to the right of the tearoom, then turn right onto the track beyond them. Walk through the gardens following **signs** pointing to Skeleton Gorge and Smuts Track, and you will come to the unmistakable **Contour Path** (**35min**). Go straight across this, past a metal plaque which shows that you're now on **Smuts Track**: from here up

Distance: 4km (2.5 mi); at least 4h

Grade: moderate to strenuous; do not attempt in wet weather; ascent of 640 m (100 ft); good shade

Risk of vertigo: minor

Equipment: strong shoes essential (walking boots *strongly recommended*), sunhat, suncream, warm clothing, wind- and waterproofs, water; walking pole(s) helpful

Transport: 🚌 blue City Sightseeing bus or taxi to Kirstenbosch Botanical Gardens. 🚗 If driving, park in the upper parking area.

Refreshments: restaurant and tearoom at the start and end; none en route

Points of interest:
Fine 'Afro-montane' forest
Rare Table Mountain flowers
Favourite walk of General Jan Smuts

was the favourite walk of General Jan Smuts (1970-1950), a Boer War hero who went on to be Prime Minister of South Africa twice. If it's any encouragement, he was still enjoying this walk in his seventies!

The well-built path now climbs up the left side of bouldery **Skeleton Gorge**, which has a trickle of running water even in the dry season. Here the tall trees are reminiscent of tropical rain forest, green and pleasantly shady, with some impressive ferns further up. The going is very steep, sometimes with rock

View just above the top of Skeleton Gorge

steps, sometimes with logs, but there are plenty of excuses to stop and look at mosses, ferns and gnarled tree trunks. The time taken to get up this section will depend on your fitness, enthusiasm and the weather, but take time to enjoy the forest. Eventually you will reach a **log ladder** beside a cliff (**1h10min**), requiring two hands to climb (stow binoculars, cameras, etc before you begin).

After the ladder, the path becomes unclear, but more-or-less ascends up the stream bed, keeping away from the cliff on the left. It's a bit of a scramble in places, but not difficult. When you reach some rock-filled, metal gabions, the path **leaves the stream bed** (**1h25min**) and veers off to the right. Follow this zigzagging path, and you will **emerge from the trees** (**1h45min**)

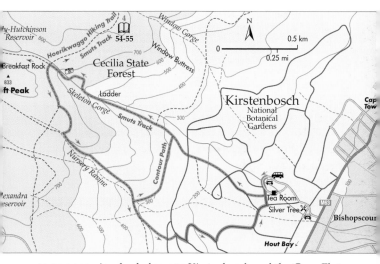

to an open view back down to Kirstenbosch and the Cape Flats beyond. Shortly after, you cross to the left bank of the stream, and just beyond this, look out for the startling red flowers of red disa orchid — 'the Pride of Table Mountain' — in late summer.

Before long you'll reach **Breakfast Rock** (under **2h**), a massive chunk that has fallen from the cliffs above, and now lies tilted on the slope. Here the path splits; take the right fork, which in a few yards leads to a National Park **information 'hub' at a 4-way junction**. (*You might consider other walks from here, but only if you have a map. The Hely-Hutchinson Reservoir is straight ahead, meeting up with Walk 7. The right fork leads to Maclear's Beacon,* *from where you could follow Walk 4 back to the upper cableway station or descend Platteklip Gorge (Walk 5).)*

However, our route back, via Nursery Ravine, uses the left fork, and starts by winding around the back of Breakfast Rock. The sandy path is a little narrow and overgrown, but still well-trodden, with a few minor scrambles over rock outcrops. Some Hollywood-type cliffs on the right are a foretaste of the weird and wonderful rock formations to come. Eventually the **path starts to drop (2h20min)**, and soon after you reach another **information 'hub'**.

The route down **Nursery Ravine** runs left from the hub,  beginning down a steep log staircase. The path beyond drops rapidly down the valley, with impressive cliffs on your left. After about 20 minutes down (**2h40min**), the sheer slopes on the right have wonderful populations of king proteas, South Africa's national flower, in bloom from February to April. Watch out for sunbirds feeding on these massive flowers, which are over 30 cm (1 ft) across (see cover photograph).

Then the path enters the welcome shade of the **forest** once more (**2h55min**), occasionally disappear-

Statue of General Jan Smuts in Company Gardens; you pass it on Walk 1.

JAN CHRISTIAN

SMUTS

Kirstenbosch Gardens, with Nursery Ravine behind to the left

ing into the stream bed, but mostly well-graded and obvious, with long sections of knee-sapping log steps. Occasional name plates on the trees shows that you are now nearing Kirstenbosch once more.

When you reach the **Contour Path** again (**3h25min**), you can either turn left, back to the 'Smuts Track' plaque at the foot of Skeleton Gorge and then right and down into Kirstenbosch, or you can turn right and then follow other signs into a different corner of Kirstenbosch. Tired but rewarded, you've earned a beer, or even a meal, in the Silver Tree Restaurant (see overleaf).

Silver Tree

For Walk 6 we recommend breakfast on the veranda of the tearoom near entrance gate 2 at the upper parking area. For dinner on the way back, aim for the excellent Silver Tree Restaurant. We've gone here straight after descending Nursery Ravine and been welcomed without a qualm, but you can always sit on the patio, admiring the sunset over the mountain, if you feel too scruffy.

'Catch of the day' at Silver Tree — in this case Cape salmon on a bed of parsley potatoes

SILVER TREE RESTAURANT
Kirstenbosch Botanic Gardens, Rhodes Avenue, Newlands, Cape Town (021 762 9585
www.kirstenboschrestaurant.com
info@kirstenboschrestaurant.com
daily 08.30-22.00
RR   (CC: V, MC, AM, DC)

The menu is varied, from **burgers** and **pasta** to excellent barbecued '**catch of the day**' and prime cut venison, served with *putu pap* (a sort of maize meal porridge), roast tomato and onion béarnaise. There are interesting **starters** and **salads**, **snack platters for two** served with mini herb pitas, tempting **sweets** and an excellent **wine** list. The Fynbos Deli next door is also worth visiting to stock up on snacks for later walks.

restaurants

eat

SWEET AND SOUR

Here are two of our favourite cold recipes — the first an interesting accompaniment for barbecued meat or fish, the other a perfect complement for South Africa's wonderful fresh fruit.

Sweet and sour carrots

Boil or steam the carrots until cooked but still firm, then drain. Arrange carrots, onions and peppers in layers, finishing with carrots. Mix all the other ingredients in a saucepan, bring to the boil and simmer 2 min, stirring constantly. Pour sauce over the carrot mix and allow to cool. Marinate covered in the fridge for two days, stirring occasionally. It keeps well for a week or so.

Fruit with red wine sauce

Should you have some left-over red wine (unlikely, we admit — you might have to open another bottle to make this and drink the left-overs …), this aromatic sauce is delicious with peaches, pears, berries and probably other fruit. Just simmer all the ingredients in an open saucepan for about 10 min. until it is syrupy. Allow to cool, then drizzle over the fruit just before serving.

Sweet and sour carrots
Ingredients (for 2 people)
500 g carrots, sliced
1 green pepper, cut into strips
1 onion, sliced
1/2 cup tomato puree
1/3 cup white vinegar
2 tbsp oil
1 tsp Worcester sauce (optional)
1/2 cup sugar
1/2 tsp prepared mustard
1/2 tsp salt
black pepper to taste

Red wine sauce
Ingredients (for 2 people)
1 cup red wine
3/4 cup sugar
3 cloves
1/4 tsp black pepper
2 tsp grated lemon peel
1 tbsp balsamic vinegar

recipes

eat

If you have little time to explore, or don't want to hire a car, this pleasant trip on the 'blue' City Sightseeing bus is a good way to see some dramatic landscapes, commuter villages and exclusive suburbs around the Cape Town peninsula — as well as to access several walks.

hout bay circuit

EXCURSION

This tour began operating in spring 2005, and already they've had to replace their buses with larger 50-seaters! It provides a convenient way to see more of the Cape Peninsula — and access for a few of our walks. Although this is the 'blue' route, note that the bus is actually *red*; however, it's a single-deck bus, not the open-topped double-deckers of the main City Sightseeing (red) route.

Timings do sometimes go slightly awry, so don't worry if the bus is a little late arriving at any stop. The guides assure us they will let passengers off between stops if requested (at Constantia Nek, for example). They say they'll also stop to pick up anyone who waves a ticket at them, even between stops, but we wouldn't recommend relying on this! The trip is better value if you use the hop-on, hop-off

Distance: about 54km (34 mi); 2h30min without stops

Equipment: money for refreshments and the various attractions en route; relevant gear for any walk

Fare: currently R100 per day, hop on or off as often as you want.

Refreshments on route: cafés and restaurants at several stops

Points of interest:
Kirstenbosch Botanic Gardens
World of Birds; admission R50
Imizamo Yethu Township R50
Kronendal farmhouse
Hout Bay Harbour
Llandudno and other beach resorts
Bakoven
Camps Bay

Blue City Sightseeing Bus Timetable (stops at Cape Town Tourism, 20 min after the Aquarium). For current times, check website: www.citysightseeing.co.za

Departs	Departs	Arrives
Aquarium	*Hout Bay*	*Aquarium*
09.45	11.20	12.00
10.45	12.20	13.00
12.00	13.40	14.20
13.00	14.40	15.20
14.20	16.05	16.45*
15.20	17.05	17.45*

* = tour ends

service to spend time at some of the stops. You also get money-off vouchers for attractions along the way with your ticket. There is a commentary (in English) on the bus, but these notes supplement what your guide might offer.

The bus **starts its circuit** outside the **Two Oceans Aquarium** on the **Victoria & Alfred (V&A) Waterfront** (although you can start from any stop and buy your ticket on the bus), and we quote timings from there. It also stops at the 1882 clock tower in the V&A, and outside Cape Town Tourism in Burg Street. It then twists through the city, past the Lord Nelson Hotel — said to be the best hotel in Africa — and onto De Waal Drive, the major highway named after Sir Frederick de Waal, Administrator of the Cape from 1910 to 1925. On the right now, rising up towards the towering rocks of the Devil's Peak, is the **Groote Schuur Estate** (the name means 'Great Barn') which was gifted to the nation by the businessman, politician and arch-colonialist Cecil Rhodes. On the left is the Groote Schuur Hospital where Professor Christian Barnard performed the world's first human heart transplant in 1967.

Just beyond this, look up the slope to your right and you may spot wildebeest and springbok introduced into a large paddock. An experiment is also underway here to 'reconstitute' a race of zebra called the *quagga* (pronounced 'kwokka') that was hunted to extinction in the 19th century, and you can sometimes spot the *quaggas* from the road. Just beyond is the **Rhodes Memorial**, a neoclassical structure designed by Herbert Baker, complete with four pairs of lion-sphinxes. Beyond that is Cape Town University, again built on land donated by Rhodes.

The bus next stops at **Kirstenbosch Botanic Gardens** (**45min**; Walk 6), a superb sylvan retreat displaying around half of South Africa's 18,000 species of flowering plants. You can get off here to explore the gardens, or have a meal or snack in the pleasant tearoom or Silver Tree Restaurant (see page 72).

The route now follows Rhodes Avenue through leafy Cecilia Forest. On your left you see some of the famous Constantia vineyards cut into the sandy hillside. The first vineyards here were laid out by the Cape governor Simon van der Stel in 1685. Soon you come to **Constantia Nek roundabout** at the top of the pass *(nek),* and straight ahead is the Constantia Nek Restaurant, one of the oldest in Cape Town (Walk 7; see page 88).

Scarlet ibis at the World of Birds

The bus now winds its way down the road to Hout Bay, a charming town which is so self-contained that in the 1980s it self-styled itself as a 'Republic'. The first stop here is at the **World of Birds** (**1h05min**), a private bird collection which includes around 300 colourful species of birds and small mammals in four hectares of land — said to be the 'largest bird park in Africa' (admission R50). Allow two-three hours if you want to walk round the complete collection.

Next the bus stops at **Kronendal** (**1h10min**), one of the

Mother and child in the Imizamo Yethu township. All people in the township share in the fees paid by tourists for the tours

oldest farmhouses in Cape Province, the foundations of which may date from 1681. This stop also gives access to the **Imizamo Yethu Township** — its Xhosi name means 'our collective struggle'. As the rainbow nation climbs out of its dark past, the dynamism of these informal townships in adversity is remarkable, and the hour-long tour is highly recommended (R60, but R50 with ticket discount). As the bus moves on, look over to the hill on the right and you'll see the 'other' Lichtenstein Castle, built as an exact replica of the one in Germany.

The bus continues down to **Hout Bay Harbour (1h35min**; Walk 8), and stops beside Mariner's Wharf, a harbour-front emporium, opened in 1984, that helped put the town on the tourist map. There's a wine store, oak smokery and pearl and artefact shops here, as well as a busy seafood bistro. If the bus is on schedule, it stops here for about 20 minutes, which gives time to visit the shops or stroll out to the pier (watch for whales in the bay in springtime). The hill at the far side of the bay is Chapman's Peak, and you can see the toll road cut into the hillside. The road was a magnificent feat of engineering by Charl Marais in 1915-1922, and has recently been extensively re-engineered and stabilised.

Even if you don't do our walks here, it's well worth extending your stop at Hout Bay between buses to explore the busy harbour. Walk along the harbourside to the Lookout Deck (see page 96). As the bus leaves Hout Bay, look up to the left and you'll see a familiar shape in unfamiliar surroundings: this hill is called the 'Little Lion's Head' for reasons that will be obvious to those that have completed Walk 3!

Now the bus comes down to the magnificent west coast, a shoreline of cliffs and rocks interspersed with beautiful beaches which are used to the full by Capetonians in summer. The first village you pass, tucked down amongst the rocks to the left, is **Llandudno**, a charming and uncommercialised holiday village (there isn't even a shop!). When it was first developed in 1903, it reminded the developer's wife of the Welsh town with the same name. Next you pass the **Oudekraal Picnic Area**. *Oude-kraal* means 'old corral', because this is where the Hottentots used to hold cattle stolen from the Dutch settlers in Cape Town. On the right, you'll pass the Twelve Apostles Hotel, named after the ridge of mountains behind. Beyond the hotel on the right is the Bellsfontein Kramat, one of a protective ring of mosques around Cape Town, and the burial place of Sheikh Noorul Mubeen.

Now the route becomes built-up as we enter the highly desirable coastal suburbs of Cape Town. First is **Bakoven**, named after a rock offshore shaped like an old-fashioned baker's oven. Next comes a stop at **Camps Bay** (**1h55min**): it's worth getting off here if you want to explore the tidal pools on the coast and the shops and restaurants along the promenade. The bus then continues past **Clifton**, with four isolated beaches divided by granite boulders. There are fabulously expensive apartment complexes along the coast here. Steep slopes are no problem for the well-to-do because many of the apartments come with their own private funiculars!

Bantry Bay, next along the coast, is another trendy suburb, followed by another bus stop at **Sea Point** (**2h05min**). If you've

The Sentinel and Hout Bay from the sea

Back at the bustle of the V&A

done nothing but sit on the bus so far, this is a good place to get off. You can walk along the seafront from Sea Point back to the V&A Waterfront in about 1h30min, although the last stretch takes you inland a bit. It's popular with local folk for its cooling sea-breezes, and there's a nice view out to Robben Island.

If you stay on the bus, you'll pass the same landmarks as you would on foot. **Three Anchor Bay** is named after the cargo nets that were once suspended here by three anchors to stop smugglers, although nets and anchors have long since gone. At **Green Point** look for the red-and-white **Mouille Point Lighthouse** — the first lighthouse in South Africa, dating back to 1824. Finally the bus brings you back to the bustle of the V&A. The last bus of the day terminates here, but others go on to the clock tower and Cape Town Tourism, if they're more convenient for where you're staying.

The walk from Constantia Nek to the Table Mountain reservoirs is a popular, but steep walk on a well-built track. You quickly escape the bustle, to a haven of peace and wildness on the 'Back Table', where you encounter some impressive Victorian engineering.

table mountain reservoirs

WALK

Before you begin this walk, check closing time of the Waterworks Museum! **The walk starts** at **Constantia Nek roundabout**, directly opposite the restaurant. Make your way through the trees in the top right-hand corner of the car park (with the road behind you), and walk a short distance up a tarmac road. A National Park sign here shows details of local walks.

Immediately inside the gate, turn left up a well-constructed flight of timber steps through the forestry plantation, quickly gaining altitude (almost all of the height gain on this walk is in this first stretch!). Turn left when you meet the **jeep track** (**15min**); follow this round one sharp right-hand bend, then

Distance: about 4km (2.5mi) *each way*; allow 3h up and 2h back.

Grade: easy but steep, with an ascent of 550 m/1800 ft; little shade

Risk of vertigo: minimal

Equipment: stout walking shoes, sunhat, suncream, wind- and waterproof clothing, water bottle

Transport: 🚌 as Excursion 1 on page 75; ask to be let off at Constantia Nek. 🚗 There is an informal car park off the roundabout directly opposite the restaurant.

Refreshments: Constantia Nek Restaurant at the start and finish; otherwise just a tap at the dam overseer's cottage (with untreated drinking water)

Points of interest:
Great views to False Bay and Table Mountain
Historic reservoirs
Waterworks Museum: 09.30-16.00 every weekend; from Nov-Apr also open 09.30-15.30 Mon-Thu and 09.30-14.00 Fri; admission free

immediately look for more steps, slightly obscured, on your left. (If you prefer, you can continue up the jeep track rather than take this steeper short-cut path, but the path is more scenic. If you stay on the track, keep left at the next two forks.)

The path (part of the **Hoerik-waggo Hiking Trail**) now climbs round the slopes of **Bel Ombre** peak (725 m). Most of the trees were harvested from this hillside in 2003, so there is little shade, but some attractive *fynbos* is developing, and you may spot some king proteas. The shade of some tall remaining trees offers a **rest spot** (**40min**). Just a little further on, you meet the jeep track again. Follow this up to the left, keeping to the concrete track at each intersection. The slope here is steep, but a fern-covered cliff offers welcome shade through most of the day and the views towards False Bay get progressively more spectacular.

Then, as you round a corner, the expanse of the **Back Table comes into sight** (**1h15min**), rising up to Maclear's Beacon beyond. The gradient now becomes much easier, and you'll see the stone wall of the first reservoir (De Villiers, built in 1907) off to your left. Soon you come across a group of neat build-

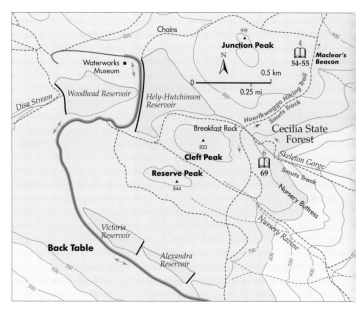

ings, including the former **dam overseer's cottage** (**1h25min**). Just beyond it, on the right, a **tap** on a concrete plinth offers what we're assured is potable water — this is the last chance to fill water bottles.

A short way further on, at a bend in the road, a neatly-built **park 'hub' with information board** shows other walking alternatives, but don't attempt these without a map. Our walk stays on the concrete track which now bends deeper into the Back Table. **Alexandra Reservoir** (**1h40min**), dating from 1903, comes up on the right. This area was once forested with non-

The hiking trail near the start of the walk, with the jeep track below and Constantia's vineyards beyond

native conifers, now felled; their gaunt skeletons litter the hillside. The track now climbs slowly past **Victoria Reservoir** (1896), then bends round to reveal impressive **Woodhead Reservoir** on your left (**2h15min**). Some tall stone pines still standing here offer welcome shade.

Construction of the Woodhead Reservoir began in 1890, with all the materials winched by cable up Kasteelsport Ravine on the west face of the mountain (Walk 2). The reservoir was opened in 1897, and its water was routed through the pipeline followed in Walk 2 to a reservoir in the city. However its supplies became inadequate for the growing city within a year of commissioning, and work began on an even larger reservoir above it — the **Hely-Hutchinson Reservoir**, opened seven years later. Continue along the track and you will cross beneath the impressive walls of this reservoir, 532 m long and with a maximum height of 15 m.

At the far side is the **Waterworks Museum**, with an old winch and a crane outside. To build the reservoir, they brought a steam engine (built in Kilmarnock, Scotland) up Kasteelsport Ravine piece by piece, and reconstructed it here, complete with

Old winch and crane beside the Hely-Hutchinson Reservoir (right), and the locomotive inside the Waterworks Museum (below)

THE CORPORATION OF THE CITY OF CAPE TOWN

a 2 km railway track. The loco is preserved inside the museum, which tells the full story of the reservoir's construction.

Note that a route is signposted to the upper cableway station across the Woodhead Reservoir dam. Don't be tempted — it involves several steep climbs and descents.

The route back is simply to retrace your steps. It's probably easier to keep on the concrete track, rather than the footpath, where it crosses below Bel Ombre (in places the concrete gives way to gravel), but watch for the final flight of steps down to the right, just beyond a junction where the concrete track does a very sharp left turn. Descend the steps back to the start, in time perhaps for a beer or meal in the **Constantia Nek Restaurant (5h)**.

Constantia Nek

This restaurant is perfectly sited for walks along the Contour Path or to the Back Table (Walk 8). It is just beside the roundabout where the M63 Rhodes Drive meets the roads to Hout Bay and Constantia (the blue City Sightseeing bus stops here on request).

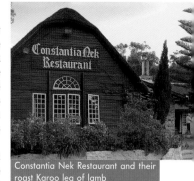

Constantia Nek Restaurant and their roast Karoo leg of lamb

The oldest restaurant in Cape Town, it dates back to 1923 and has the feel of an alpine *stübe*. It serves **breakfast** until 11.30, **lunch** from 12.00-15.00, **tea and scones** in the afternoon, and **dinner** from 18.00, either indoors or on the pleasant garden terrace. But it sometimes closes for private parties, so check before your walk if you want dinner on your return.

The roast Karoo-raised leg of lamb is delicious, as is the ostrich fillet with a port and black cherry sauce. Healthier options include hot Greek salad, crocodile salad and line-caught fish of the day.

CONSTANTIA NEK RESTAURANT
1 Hout Bay Road, Constantia
(021 794 5132
www.constantianek.co.za
restaurant@constantianek.co.za
Mon-Fri 10.00-late; Sat/Sun 09.00-late
RR   (CC: V, MC, AM, DC)

restaurants

eat

Braais are a Cape Town speciality. This recipe was inspired by a little book we found called *What's on the Braai?* by Ina Paarman. Supermarkets sell *braai* packs of chops and steaks ready-marinated. If you can't find 'branded' seasonings, just improvise. If you are invited to a *braai,* take along something to cook and share, and maybe a side salad (see pages 51 and 73).

Braaied chicken sosaties

Sosaties are of Malay origin, and are cubes of curry-marinated meat threaded onto wooden skewers with onions and dried apricots or peaches. Traditionally cubes of sheep's tail fat, known as 'speck', were also added.

If you are using the very dry variety of dried fruit (as opposed to the plump, ready-to-eat version), pour boiling water over and leave to stand a few minutes. Then drain and cover. Mix the curry sauce or paste with coconut milk, add the cubed meat and marinate overnight.

Next day make up skewers by threading meat, fruit and onion alternately. Season lightly. *Braai* or grill, turning frequently, and baste with the remaining sauce. Bring any remaining sauce to the boil and serve with the *sosaties*. Good with plain rice and a salad.

Ingredients (for 2 people)
2 chicken breasts, cubed (or lamb or pork)
dried peaches or apricots (you can also use tinned)
Tikka curry coat & cook sauce, or curry paste
1/2 tin coconut milk
1 onion, quartered and separated into 'leaves'
sosatie sticks or skewers

recipes

eat

This easy, scenic walk leads you round Karbonkelberg Peak to the ruins of a 1944 radar station with dramatic vistas along the coastline to Lion's Head and a novel back-to-front view of Table Mountain. Be warned that the walk can be tiring in hot weather.

hout bay to karbonkelberg

WALK

If you do this walk using the blue City Sightseeing bus (see Excursion 1), note that you will need to take one of the earliest buses to complete the walk and get the last bus back!

The walk mostly follows a well-graded track; remember that track-walking can seem a bit unremitting in hot weather. Note, too, that the walk is undergoing change. Major work is in progress to clear non-native trees from the upper slopes of Karbonkelberg. Although this is removing welcome shade, it should lead to good regeneration of the natural *fynbos* vegetation. As the trees are removed, other work may be done on the track, so watch out for possible changes.

If you **start the walk** from

Distance: 6.2km (3.5 mi) each way: allow at least 2h30min up and 2h down

Grade: easy, but little shelter in hot weather; ascent of 595 m (1950 ft)

Risk of vertigo: minor

Equipment: walking shoes, sunhat, suncream, warm clothing and water-proofs, water

Transport: 🚌 as Excursion 1 on page 75; alight at Hout Bay (earliest bus out recommended). 🚗 If you are travelling by car, you can drive to the top of Bayview Road (see walking instructions below) and park on the roadside just before the gate, which should be safe, but make sure you are not blocking any driveways.

Refreshments: Mariner's Wharf Restaurant, iKhaya Coffee Bar and Lookout Deck Restaurant (page 96) on the harbour at the start and end; none en route, and no reliable water

Points of interest:
Dramatic coastal scenery
Ruined World War II radar station
A 'different' view of Table Mountain.

the bus stop at **Mariner's Wharf in Hout Bay**, walk down past the restaurant, then turn right along the harbour front. The **South African Fisheries Museum** is worth a visit (admission R5; open 08.00-16.00, weekdays only). Further along the

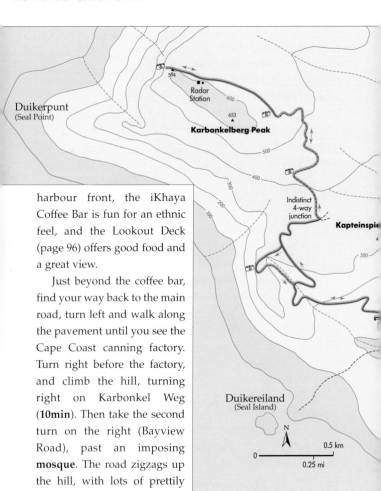

harbour front, the iKhaya Coffee Bar is fun for an ethnic feel, and the Lookout Deck (page 96) offers good food and a great view.

Just beyond the coffee bar, find your way back to the main road, turn left and walk along the pavement until you see the Cape Coast canning factory. Turn right before the factory, and climb the hill, turning right on Karbonkel Weg (**10min**). Then take the second turn on the right (Bayview Road), past an imposing **mosque**. The road zigzags up the hill, with lots of prettily named side streets, but the main Bayview Road is always evident. A gate at the top of Bayview, beside a **'Karbonkelberg' National Park sign** (**35min**), marks the beginning of the walk proper.

The track beyond the sign rises steadily, until a **stream** crosses the track (**50min**). A little beyond this, there is a hairpin bend in the track, and perhaps a little shade from cliffs on the left. Then (**1h**) the gravel track gives way to a much sandier surface, with an obvious turning place on the left. Karbonkelberg Peak (653 m) is now directly ahead.

Continue up this sandy track, consolidated with brash in places to stop erosion. The edges of the track are especially colourful with flowers in spring. Eventually the well-made track gives way to a sandy, **double tyre track** (**1h10min**). Continue up this for about three more minutes, until there's a low, rocky peak just ahead on the right. Now watch for an **indistinct four-way intersection** — the most difficult bit of route-finding on the entire walk. Turn left here on the strongest path, heading

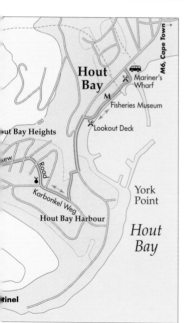

Hout Bay

Mariner's Wharf

M6, Cape Town

M Fisheries Museum

Lookout Deck

ut Bay Heights

ew Road

100

Karbonkel Weg

Hout Bay Harbour

York Point

Hout Bay

tinel

The route back follows the valley bottom here, heading towards The Sentinel.

roughly towards Karbonkelberg, and keep uphill. In a few places it is obvious that this was once a vehicle track, but erosion has cut *dongas* (gullies) to a depth of a metre or more along most of its length, and only a path remains.

When the path bends right above an obvious **flat-topped rock (1h20min)**, it becomes more stable. The original track to the radar station was consolidated with building rubble, so the key from now on is to 'follow the orange brick road' as it zigzags steadily up the hill! At the point where the the **summit marker of Karbonkelberg is high above you to the left** (**1h40min**), you get an amazing back-to-front vista of Table Mountain — like every other view but in 'mirror image', with the cableway clearly silhouetted at the *left-hand* end! Soon after, Lion's Head also comes into sight. The track flattens out (**1h50min**) and, shortly after, you reach the **radar buildings**. Continue past them to the end of the track, where a sandy path leads off right towards a rocky promontory. This is a perfect picnic spot, with spectacular views past Llandudno to Clifton, Camps Bay and Lion's Head beyond.

The walk back is mostly a matter of retracing your steps; some 50 minutes down, remember to look for the narrow sandy track which leads to the **four-way intersection**, avoiding the erosion gully, then turn right on the sandy vehicle track. About five minutes after this, an obvious sandy track branches off to the right and steeply downhill towards a low col at the coast. As a pleasant detour, follow this track down and head to the col for spectacular cliff views (but watch for the sheer edge!). Then retrace your steps a short way and take a narrow sandy path which follows the line of the stream down the valley. Descend this carefully, and you will soon pick up the main track downhill again.

Even with this detour, two hours will bring you from the radar station back to the **harbourside at Hout Bay** (**4h30min**).

Lookout Deck

Mariner's Wharf is the better-known eatery beside Hout Bay Harbour, and it's great if you like boy waiters in sailor suits, but it's quite touristy and often busy. We prefer the more relaxed pace at the Lookout Deck at the other end of the harbour — with fantastic views from its wooden deck across the harbour to Chapman's Peak. It's perfectly sited for Walk 8, although you'll need to check the time for the last City Sightseeing bus if you came that way (or pay R2 to park your car on the harbour-front).

The **seafood** menu is especially varied and tempting — try the chilli and orange calamari or one of the groaning seafood platters; some evenings there's a seafood *braai*. There are interesting **salads** and **meat** dishes too: we enjoyed the lamb knuckle curry. Hearty **breakfasts** are served at weekends.

LOOKOUT DECK
Harbour waterfront, Hout Bay
(021 790 0900
www.dining-out.co.za/member_
    details.asp?MemberID=2451
lookoutdeck@elkomsa.net
Mon-Fri   10.00-23.00,   Sat/Sun/
    public holidays 09.00-23.00
RR   (CC: V, MC, AM, DC)

Enjoy a lamb knuckle curry right at the water's edge.

restaurants

eat

Everyday Malay meals, *bredies* are spicy stews of meat and various vegetables, and are named after the main vegetable ingredient. *Bredies* are easy to make, but often use the cheaper (tastier) cuts of meat which benefit from slow simmering.

Tomato *bredie*

Tomato *bredie*

This tomato bredie recipe doesn't take too long to cook, depending on the quality of the beef, and tastes best made with fresh tomatoes.

Blanch, skin and pulp the fresh tomatoes. Chop the onions and chilli, peel and halve or quarter the potatoes (depending on size), slice the pepper.

Heat oil in a large saucepan and brown the meat and onions. Add all the other ingredients except the turmeric and masala to the pan, and cook for 20 min.

Now add the remaining spices and simmer, uncovered, until the meat is tender. Serve with rice and perhaps a *sambal* (see recipe on page 137).

Ingredients (for 2 people)
500 g stewing beef
oil for frying
1 onion, chopped
stock cube
250 g fresh tomatoes (or use tinned)
2 tsp tomato paste (only 1 tsp if using tinned tomatoes)
1 tsp salt
1 tbsp sugar
1 green chilli, chopped
1/4 green pepper, sliced
500 g small potatoes
1/2 tsp turmeric
1/2 tsp leaf masala

recipes

eat

This train journey offers views of Table Mountain and spectacular coastal scenery. It's a good way to get to Walks 9-11, or you could combine it with a wander through Simon's Town (see Walk 11) or follow the 'cat-walk' — the shoreline promenade from St James back to Muizenberg, where you can reboard the train.

simon's town by train

EXCURSION

It's a special treat to travel on this historic railway line, construction of which began in 1864 and was completed in 1890. Cecil Rhodes was one of the passengers on the first train to complete this journey. Trains leave every 50 minutes, but we suggest selecting one of the trains with the Biggsy's restaurant carriage (named after train robber Ronald Biggs), so you can have breakfast, lunch or just a snack as you travel. Travelling in this carriage (which doesn't operate on Mondays) also provides extra security as there are always staff on hand.

The route (shown on the inside back cover) is remarkable because over 22 miles there are 28 stations: the shortest scheduled time between stations is just one minute (between Rosebank and Rondebosch — a distance of only 800 metres), and the

Distance: 35 km (22mi) each way; under 1h10min

Equipment: money for refreshments and shopping; any gear for walking (see relevant walk)

Fare: R12 single for the complete route (if you wish to break the journey, you need to buy two separate tickets).

Refreshments on route: Biggsy's Restaurant Car; restaurants in Simon's Town and Muizenberg

Points of interest:
Historic railway route
Views to Devil's Peak and Muizenberg Peak
False Bay and its beaches

Trains with Biggsy's restaurant car, timetable (for up-to-date times see www.capemetrorail.co.za)

Departs Cape Town		Departs Simon's Town	
Tuesdays–Fridays (not Mondays)			
05.50	15.06	07.08	16.30
08.40	17.48	10.02	19.11
12.00		13.20	
Saturdays			
05.55	12.05	07.13	13.58
08.47	15.36	10.10	17.14
Sundays and holidays			
08.30	11.25	09.55	14.54

Simon's Town station is the end of the line (seen here with a colourful education train visiting). Below: as well as the restaurant, the Biggsy's carriage also has a bar, popular with regular customers.

longest five minutes. So there's plenty time to take in the scenery! The right-hand side of the train has the better views for the first half of the trip out of Cape Town, but it is better to be on the left after Steenberg.

Leaving **Cape Town station**, you might catch a glimpse of the Castle of Good Hope on the right. Within a mile you come to **Woodstock**, once called Papendorp after Pieter van Papendorp, an 18th-century local Dutch farmer. The next stop is **Salt River**, originally named Zout Rivier by the Dutch because of its salinity. You now have nice views up to Table Mountain on the right, with the more isolated Devil's Peak at its leftmost end. **Observatory** is one of the more historically interesting suburbs of Cape Town, named after the Royal Observatory that was built there by the British Admiralty in 1827. At **Mowbray** and just before **Rosebank**, if you look up to Table Mountain, you might glimpse the elaborate temple-like memorial to Cecil Rhodes, who was Prime Minister of the Cape Colony from 1890. The ruin clinging to Devil's Peak behind the Rhodes Memorial is the King's Blockhouse, used to send signal messages between Cape Town and Muizenberg before the development of the electric telegraph in 1860.

Just beyond the university suburb of **Rondebosch**, you get a brief view on the left across the famous **Newlands** Cricket Ground — perhaps enough to see a ball being bowled if there is a game on! Next we reach **Claremont** station, the first station to be completed when the line was opened in 1864. The train now begins to climb a little, past **Harfield Road**, **Kenilworth** (with its race-course) to **Wynberg** — the highest station on the line at an altitude of 50 m. You are now 13 km from the start of your journey! **Wittebome** is apparently named after the Silver Trees that once grew there. On your right, you are looking over towards Constantia and the winelands. **Plumstead** station was built partly for the transport of fruit from the Constantia Valley. Just after **Steurhof**, the line crosses a shallow stream called the

Diep River with a station of the same name. **Heathfield** is an interchange with the Cape Flats railway line. A little beyond, **Retreat** is named after a series of advances and retreats during the Battle of Muizenberg between Dutch and British troops in 1795. It marks approximately the half-way point on the line. The dramatic mountains ahead are rough and rocky. By 1657, the Dutch had given them the name of Stone Mountains, still recorded in the name of the next station, **Steenberg**.

The 'action' now switches to the left of the train. The line crosses the northern end of **Zandvlei**, a large estuary teaming with bird life and popular as a boating area, hence the station of **Lakeside**! The next stop, **Valsbaai** (False Bay) is just a little short of the beautiful coastal inlet of that name, along which the rest of the line winds. Early Portuguese mariners often mistakenly thought that the rocky point at the eastern end of the bay, Cape Hangklip, was Cape Point and so they turned north too soon, only to find they were in a navigational cul-de-sac — False Bay.

As the train approaches **Muizenberg**, you have a wonderful view along one of the longest beaches in the world, stretching for 40 km. Watch for surfers trying to crest the breakers that sweep onto the beach here. Over a century ago, the goldfield millionaires of southern Africa flocked to Muizenberg as one of the area's top seaside resorts. Today, its Victorian glory looks a little faded, but major renovation is underway.

The redbrick station at Muizenberg was designed by Sir Herbert Baker and opened in 1913. The station has a restaurant, but we prefer to go round the corner to the Empire Café (page 112). Other buildings overlooking the railway on the right include the Posthuys, which was built in 1673 as a signal house and is South Africa's oldest surviving European house, and a shocking-pink Italianate building that is now the Natalia Labia Museum, with a range of old masters from the National Gallery.

The train now trundles along the rocky shoreline to **St James.** You'll pass an elaborate, privately-owned thatched house between the train and the shore on your left, and immediately afterwards you'll see two more thatched houses on your right. The second of these is where Cecil Rhodes died in 1902, now a museum (which can be visited from the coastal promenade). St James was originally a simple halt beside St James Church, but it became so popular that the church was demolished in 1900, and replaced by a new church across the road, to make way for a bigger station retaining the original name. Note the gaily-painted bathing huts by the shore here. (On your return, you could break your journey here, and walk back along the 'catwalk' promenade to Muizenberg station.)

Less than a mile on is **Kalk Bay**. Shells used to be collected from the shore here and burnt to make whitewash and mortar for buildings — *kalk* is Afrikaans for lime. The attractive harbour here includes a busy quayside fish market and several nice restaurants, but we prefer the quirky fun of Cafe Olympia along the road (see page 120).

The train now continues along the coast through **Clovelly** to **Fish Hoek**, a charming seaside town with a popular beach. Its family values are emphasised by the fact that the town is one of the few 'dry' municipalities in South Africa — no alcohol can be sold within its bounds. The train next stops at the unmanned

Kalk Bay Harbour

halt of **Sunny Cove**: note the houses perched on stilts on the slope above. Then you pass a large quarry on the right, from which most of the naval base at Simon's Town was constructed, before coming to the station for the small community of **Glencairn**. The wetland on the right just before the station is a bird sanctuary, and on the left there's a fine view across to the naval base at Simon's Town. Watch for whales in springtime.

Continuing on, the neat whitewashed cottage on the right is called Klein Vishoek, and just beyond it you will see the guns of the Lower North Battery, a reminder, like the ominous grey warships in the harbour, of the area's naval associations. Finally the train pulls into **Simon's Town**. Walk 11 describes more of the history of this naval community.

This lovely, circular walk takes you high above the busy coast road at Muizenberg to a quiet, undisturbed botanical paradise amongst weird, weather-sculpted, white calcareous rocks — complete with the dramatic Muizenberg Cave, which you can explore.

mimetes valley
WALK

It's best to do this walk between Thursdays and Saturdays, so you can end with dinner at the Empire Café (it closes at 16.00 the rest of the week). **Start the walk** at **Muizenberg station**: turn right along the main road for a short distance and cross by the 'robots' (traffic lights). Turn left up School Road, just before the car park. When you reach the **police station**, divert right into the park, walk up the grassy slope, then turn left on a gravel path.

This narrow path zigzags

Distance: 7km (4.5 mi); allow 4h

Grade: moderate on slopes (ascent of 450 m (1480 ft); easy on top; occasional shade

Equipment: stout walking shoes; sunhat, suncream, warm clothing and waterproofs, water

Transport: 🚂 to Muizenberg (see Excursion 2, page 99). 🚗 Park in the car park just before the station on the right (coming from Cape Town) or on Boyes Drive by the Bailey's Kloof sign.

Refreshments: Empire Café (see page 112 or the station restaurant at the start and end; none en route

Points of interest:
Fine *fynbos* with unusual plants
Dramatic scenery and views
Accessible limestone cave

up to Boyes Drive (**10min**). Turn left and follow the pavement for about five minutes. Cross the road at the large **Bailey's Kloof footpath sign** (motorists could park here), and go straight up the steps by the sign. A few minutes later, go straight across a contouring path. When you meet a second crossing path (**25min**), turn right, then turn left after just a few metres, and go up the steep stone steps into **Bailey's Kloof**. It's a 10- to 15-minute slog up the steps, but the view improves all the time, so there are plenty of excuses for stopping!

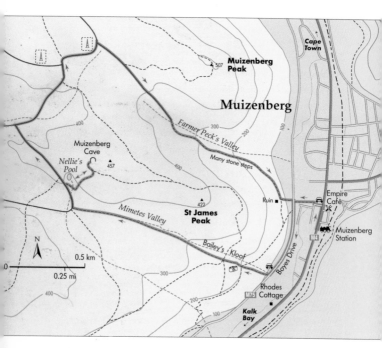

Eventually (**40min**) the path becomes a more gentle upward slope. Other paths meet it, but keep heading upwards into the valley beyond, past a couple of fence posts marking a small stream (or stream bed in the dry season). You're now in the **Mimetes Valley**, named after the *Mimetes* trees around you. These are a member of the protea family, also called the 'tree pagoda', with beautiful rosy-coloured flowers from June to November. In springtime also look beside the path for a

The *Mimetes* trees in the eponymous valley flower from June to November.

greenish heather, called *Erica urna-viridis*. The hills above Muizenberg are the only place where it's found.

The path gradually moves right, away from the floor of the valley, and in places it's cut deep into the sand by erosion. Cross a stream(bed) and a stretch of open *fynbos*, and you'll reach a wide gravel track (**1h**). Take the right fork here, then, five minutes later, look for a small sandy path with log steps that hairpins sharply back to the right (just before you reach Nellie's Pool). It's worth a diversion up here to visit the cave. Follow this path for nearly 10 minutes, through a jumble of boulders and rock outcrops, to the top of the ridge, and **Muizenberg Cave (1h15min)** is on your right. It may take a little searching for, as there is a maze of small paths around it, but the large entrance is obvious. The cave is a shady spot for a lunch break — as is Nellie's Pool, which follows.

Muizenberg Cave

Retrace your steps to the main gravel track, turn right, and **Nellie's Pool** is just a minute on, to the right (**1h25min**). It's surprising to see a pool here, even in the dry season, and if you approach quietly you might spot frogs around the edges before they plop into the water. An overhanging tree shades this alternative lunch spot.

Starting off again, the gravel track continues upwards for a short distance, then begins to descend. When you come to a **T-junction (1h40min)**, turn right. Soon you'll reach a fenced-in **military mast (1h55min)**. Follow the track round to the right in front of the enclosure, and just beyond it, take a right fork. This gravel track gives way to a sandy track **(2h05min)**. Follow this as it narrows to a footpath and leads down into **Farmer Peck's Valley**.

The path down the valley starts off reasonably gently, but soon gives way to a steep, well-constructed flight of stone steps — which is why we recommend the walk this way round! Eventually the path levels out **(3h)** and contours round to the right. At time of writing this area had been recently burnt and finding the path was a little difficult. However continue around the contour until you reach a **ruin** on the right. Turn down the stone steps on the left here, to drop back down to Boyes Drive in a few minutes.

Turn right along Boyes Drive. Continue along this for about 300 metres if you left your car at the Bailey's Kloof sign, or turn left down the path you came up from **Muizenberg** (about **4h**). York Road, for the Empire Café, is just a little to the left from the foot of School Road.

Empire Café

This takes a little finding, but *do* make the effort. From Muizenberg station, walk back into town and it's down the second street on the right; there's car parking in the square at the end. (Ignore the 'Empire' name emblazoned on the seafront, which marks the long-gone restaurant from which it took its name). Dave Jones opened this café in late 2002. The laid-back atmosphere (you could imagine it run by surfers from the nearby beach) belies the quality and presentation of the food.

Breakfasts are amazing (super **omelettes**, **filled croissants**) — a perfect start for Walk 9. Plan your walk for Thursday to Saturday, and you can have dinner too. The chalkboard menu is intriguing, with interesting **soups** and **salad starters**, **pastas**, **risottos** and delicious **lamb shanks**. Many dishes use cream and flour, but they're adaptable if you ask. Upstairs is nicest, with views over the railway to False Bay.

Empire salads: feta and butternut squash, pear and gorgonzola

Dave gave us this chicken recipe, but Michael is responsible for the bad pun in the added '(A)'. Sue's scaled-down version for two people was delicious, despite the fact that she couldn't find garlic ginger paste (she used chopped garlic and grated fresh ginger).

EMPIRE CAFÉ
11 York Road, Muizenberg
(021 788 1250
www.caperestaurants.co.za/
clients/EmpireCafe/Empire
Cafe.html
dave@my.co.za
Thu–Sat   07.00–late;   Sun–Wed
09.00–16.00
R   (CC: V, MC, AM, DC)

restaurants

eat

(A)frikkin' chickin'

Preheat oven to 180°C. Wash the apple, potato and sweet potato; peel the onions. Quarter and core the apple. Mix half the oil with curry powder, garlic ginger paste and most of the sugar. Massage the paste into the chicken pieces.

Meanwhile, par boil the potatoes and sweet potatoes in salted water. Let cool and slice into thick rounds.

Place the chicken portions in a baking dish, season, drizzle with oil, and splash with vinegar. Surround with the onions and apples, cover with foil and bake for 30 min. Then remove from oven, turn the chicken over, dust with more sugar and a little vinegar, and cook for a further 20 min or until done.

When the chicken is done, remove from the baking dish, together with apples and onions, and keep warm. Put the potato slices in the chicken juices and return the baking dish to the oven for about 15 min, to finish cooking.

Place the chicken pieces on top of the potatoes and surround with the onions and apples. Spoon the remaining sauce over and drizzle with a little honey —preferably the local *fynbos* variety.

Ingredients (for 2 people)

2 large chicken pieces
1 apple
6 pickling onions (or 1/2 onion sliced)
1 potato
1 sweet potato (orange variety)
salt
1 tsp curry powder
1 tbsp demerara sugar
1 tbsp spirit vinegar
1 tsp garlic ginger paste
2 tsp olive/sunflower oil
Runny honey to serve

recipes

eat

This attractive circular walk begins at Kalk Bay Station and leads you up the rugged mountainside, through weirdly sculpted rock scenery and two enchanted ancient remnants of Afro-montane forest. You can even have a picnic in the Amazon Forest!

the amphitheatre and echo valley

WALK

Starting from the Kalk Bay station car park, cross the road and take the obvious, wide flight of steps directly opposite. At the top of the steps, turn left along Duignam Weg for a few metres, then pick up another set of uphill steps, to emerge on Boyes Drive. Bear slightly left and cross the busy road to the **Echo Valley sign** (**5min**; motorists should be able to park here). Beside the sign, climb more stone steps, then follow the path to the right, heading towards Muizenberg.

Distance: 6km (3.5 mi); around 4h

Grade: moderate on the slopes, with an ascent of 500 m (1640 ft); easy on top; reasonable shade

Equipment: stout walking shoes, sunhat, suncream, warm clothing and waterproofs, water

Transport: 🚃 to Kalk Bay (see Excursion 2 on page 99). 🚗 Park on Boyes Drive beside the Echo Valley sign, directly above Kalk Bay harbour (the 5min-point in the walk).

Refreshments: Olympia Café at the start and end, otherwise none

Points of interest:
Ancient trees in Spes Bona Valley
The 'Amazon Forest'
Dramatic rock scenery and caves

The path here has welcome level stretches and shade from overhanging bushes. There are good views down through the trees to Kalk Bay Harbour, and to Simon's Town further round to the south. The path crosses a **stream** (**15min**), then rises beside the stream on yet another steep flight of steps. Soon the path and stream turn inland, and the craggy Ridge Peak (502m) appears in the distance. Then you reach a junction and sign at 'Weary Willy's' (**30min**). Turn right here, over the stream (you'll eventually return down the other path).

Carry on up stone steps, passing some rock shelters on your right. To the left, Echo Valley, in the rocky hollow between

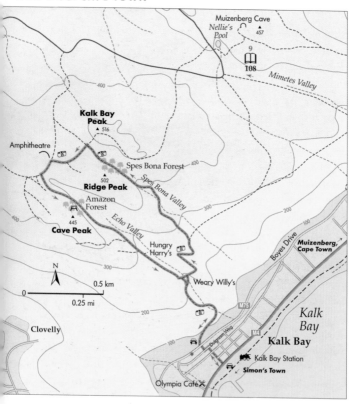

Ridge Peak and Cave Peak (445 m) further to the left, marks your route home. Resist several side paths, keeping to the main path until you reach a **signpost** (**1h**). Take the option signed 'Spes Bona Forest: 970 m', bearing slightly left. The footpath now does a wide zig, with expansive views of False Bay, before moving inland up the side of the **Spes Bona Valley**. *Spes Bona*, meaning 'Good Hope', is also the motto of Cape Town. At **another sign** (**1h10min**), turn left for the 'Forest', now encouragingly signed as only **2**00 m further on!

A steady climb for the next 15 minutes will bring you to the base of the forest. Take note of the 'keep to the path' signs; these unique fragments of forest of milkwood, yellow wood and other indigenous trees have been suffering from walker erosion, and the park authorities have gone to great expense to provide a boardwalk to prevent further damage. Please stick to it: the alternative is to close off the forests altogether to walkers, which would be a great shame, as they are magical places. On a hot day the cool shade beneath the dense canopy of leaves is very welcome, and you will want to linger amongst the twisted branches and gnarled trunks. The huge boulders surrounding the forest help to protect it from fire.

Boardwalk in Spes Bona Forest

After 20 minutes or so absorbing the atmosphere, you will be chilled enough to welcome the sun again, when you emerge from the shade, passing under a **last huge boulder (1h45min)** and a cliff dripping with water and mosses on the right. Soon after, turn left up a rocky path, following a sign pointing to the 'Amphitheatre'. This rises to a flat sandy area, where you should keep right, heading towards the view of Kommetjie and Noordhoek Beach. Soon its far wall appears ahead, and you descend into the **Amphitheatre (2h15min)**. The sculpted limestone gets stranger and stranger, with pits and holes like giant rock dough left to rise for too long. The sandy base of the amphitheatre is a good place for a break.

Then follow the 'Echo Valley Forest: 600 m' sign out of the mouth of the amphitheatre, where several indistinct tracks weave downhill; head towards Echo Valley to the left. From here the valley looks almost identical to Spes Bona, with a mini-forest in a hollow framed by twin peaks. As you descend towards this, another sign confirms the route through the

Eroded limestone above the Amphitheatre

trees, known locally as '**Amazon Forest**' (**2h35min**). Another boardwalk eases your way downwards, and there's a lovely picnic clearing off to the right.

Past the forest, the path descends through fields of sculpted boulders, some of them huge. They lie haphazardly, having apparently fallen from the craggy cliffs above. Ignore a path joining from the right, signposted '**Jojulu**' (**3h15min**). A few minutes later, a small path to the left leads to several huge boulders piled together, and it's worth a little detour to walk beneath this natural shelter known as **Hungry Harry's**. Return to the main path, and soon you'll be back at **Weary Willy's** (**3h35min**).

From here, the scent of cooking from the many eateries in Kalk Bay might speed your descent. Take care, the path is steep and rocky in places. You'll reach Boyes Drive 20 minutes down-hill and then the main street and **station at Kalk Bay** (**4h**). Turn right for just 200 metres along Main Road if you want to eat at the Olympia Café (page 120), but remember to check the time of your last train back.

Olympia Café and Deli

Kenneth McClarty's café is endearingly ramshackled, with job-lot tables and wobbly chairs, but that makes it perfect before or after a walk into Echo Valley.

You might begin with a **breakfast** of omelette (perhaps with ricotta, peppadew and rocket), ciabattas fresh from the on-site bakery, and great coffee.

OLYMPIA CAFÉ AND DELI
134 Main Road, Kalk Bay
(021 788 6396
olympia@my.co.za
daily 07.00-21.00
RRR   (CC: V, MC, DC)

Goats' cheese salad at Olympia; see their gorgonzola sirloin on page 7.

Booking isn't possible, and **queues often form for dinner** (served from 18.00). So come back from your walk at 5-ish, grab a table, have a coffee or beer, and wait until they're ready to serve. The chalkboard menu changes daily, but includes **soups** like French onion or chilled avocado, unusual

salads, **pastas** and **fish** fresh from the harbour opposite, all cooked in front of you (sauces can be left off on request). Remember that the last train back to Cape Town leaves Kalk Bay rather early, but it's only a five-minute walk to the station.

restaurants

eat

Braaied (barbecued) fish

Fish is best cooked straight from the sea. If you can't catch your own, the next best thing is to take the train from Cape Town and buy the catch of the day from the quayside at Kalk Bay harbour, maybe after doing Walk 10.

Fish are excellent *braaied*, preferably in an oiled, hinged grid or cage that can be closed on the fish while you turn it, so it doesn't fall apart. The freshest fish needs only the simplest baste to keep it moist, just butter or oil, lemon juice and seasoning (double the oil if you omit butter). For a change try this apricot baste, good with snoek.

Mix all the baste ingredients together. Open up the fish so it lies flat (or get the seller to 'vlek' the fish for you for a few extra rand). Baste, then barbecue white-side down for a few minutes over hot coals until sealed. Turn over and cook over lower heat for about 20 min, basting frequently. Season to taste.

Popular served with sweet potatoes baked in foil. Or try the butternut squash salad (see page 51).

Ingredients (for 2 people)
fresh snoek

Apricot baste:
3 tbsp melted butter
3 tbsp cooking oil
1 tbsp apricot jam
1 tbsp lemon juice
1 clove garlic, crushed
salt & black pepper

recipes

eat

This is an easy town walk, with lots on offer including history, sailors, penguins, coastal scenery and a lunch-time calamari! The timing fits well with the return train journey from Cape Town (see Excursion 2) — and there's even time to be on the beach or have a quick swim.

simon's town to boulders beach

WALK

Simon's Town has a long history. Governor Simon van der Stel discovered the bay while exploring the Cape Peninsula around 1678 and named it after himself. In 1741, the Dutch East India Company decided that Simon's Bay would be the perfect winter anchorage for their ships, and the town was founded to supply them. After the British occupation in 1806, the main base of the Royal Navy was moved here from Cape Town, and it remained the Royal Navy base until 1957 when the dockyard was handed over to the South African Navy. The British influence here is still very strong, as you will see.

Distance: 3 km (1.5 mi) *each way;* allow 2h plus plenty of time for stops

Grade: easy walking on pavements

Equipment: 'sensible' shoes, sun-hat, warm clothing and waterproofs, money for admissions, swimsuits if you fancy a dip

Transport: 🚌 to Simon's Town (see Excursion 2 on page 99). Or 🚗: park near the railway station.

Refreshments on route: ample restaurants and shops; we recommend Boulders Beach Restaurant (page 128) at the end of the outward leg

Points of interest:
Simon's Town Museum: 09.00-16.00 weekdays; 09.00-13.00 Saturdays; 09.00-15.00 Sundays and holidays; admission R5
Historic buildings along main street
African penguin colony at Boulders Beach (admission R15)

Start the walk from Simon's Town **railway station**: turn left past the Teddy Bear Shop. You'll soon pass an extensive garden on your left, with a replica figurehead of *HMS Flora* standing between two Portuguese cannons. This is the garden of

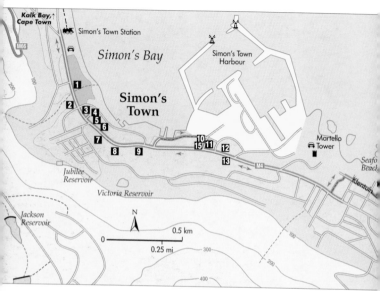

Admiralty House (1), originally built in 1743, but extensively altered in 1853 to become the official residence of the Commander-in-Chief. Today it houses the Chief of the South African Navy. Just a little beyond on the right, set up the hill slightly, is a neat white building with a rectangular gable and a pergola. Its name is **Studland** (2), after the village in Dorset. This was originally built in 1797 as a wine-house to attract sailors away from the drunken excesses of the harbour, and later included a brewery. In 1969 it was declared the town's first National Monument.

When you come to **St Francis of Assisi Parish Church** on

SIMON'S TOWN

1 Admiralty House
2 Studland
3 St Francis of Assisi
4 Simon's Town Museum
5 Naval Museum
6 St George's
7 Lord Nelson Inn
8 African Station Club
9 British Hotel
10 Sculpture Garden
11 Heritage Museum
12 Dutch Reformed Church
13 Catholic Church
14 Boulders Visitor Centre
15 Warrior Toy Museum

Studland and (below) the replica pub in Simon's Town Museum

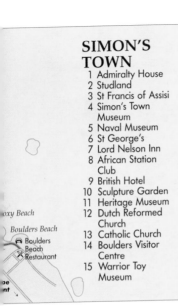

your left (3; **5min**), turn left, past the faded grandiosity of **Fleet Command HQ**, to the **Simon's Town Museum** (4) at the foot of a short cul-de-sac. It is the former residency of the governor of the Dutch East India Company, built in 1777 but extensively altered since. Displays inside illustrate the history of the town. It's worth exploring for the story of Just Nuisance, a Great Dane who was enlisted as an able seaman during World War Two, and a fascinating replica pub.

Head back to the main street, turn left, and you'll pass a **museum** on the history of the South African Navy, then look over the wall at the **St George's Dockyard Church** (6), with its clock tower. It was built as a sail-loft in 1814, and consecrated as a church in 1945. The tower in the harbour once supported an aerial ropeway that carried supplies to the Naval Hospital at the top of the hill. The strong British influence is evident on the right as you walk on: the **Lord Nelson Inn** (7), complete with the Trafalgar Bar. A little beyond on the right is the **African Station Club** of 1873 (8; now a naval reference library), and the appropriately-faded **British Hotel** (9), built in 1898.

Just past the hotel, turn left down Wharf Street to the **harbour**, with pleasant seafront restaurants. Walk in front of the restaurants to the brick steps at the far end, then through the car park, and you will come to the 'Bronze Age Sculpture Garden' (10) with some interesting artworks. Now follow the road round, past a **Heritage Museum** (11), and back up to the main road. Turn left and continue out of town.

As you walk up the hill, you will pass on your left the **Dutch Reformed Church** (12; built in 1856 and now a national monument), a **Roman Catholic church** (13) and the utilitarian military architecture of the **dockyard** and **naval base**. At least you now get some shade from a fine grove of eucalypts. Just beyond them, at the pedestrian 'robots' (traffic lights), turn left down the steps of **Whalers Way**.

Seaforth Beach straight ahead is a safe spot for a cooling swim. Otherwise, turn right beyond the public conveniences, passing some street stalls, then follow the 'penguin' signposts along narrow Kleintuin Road. Pass the Boulders Visitor Centre for now (you'll return later). As you continue along the leafy track, you may see penguins beneath the bushes on the left, and look out for dassies, too (see page 55). On the left, the sheltered cove with massive, rounded boulders is appropriately named **Boulders Beach** — another nice swimming spot, but with a

African penguins at Boulders Beach

small admission charge. You'll soon come to a car park, and just above this is Boulders Beach Restaurant (see overleaf), the perfect spot for a relaxing calamari lunch.

Our return trip follows the same route, with minor variations. Afternoon is a better time to visit the **Boulders Visitor Centre** (14) and its colony of over 3000 African penguins, resident here most of the year. From the Visitor Centre take the path straight ahead for a boardwalk overlooking the main nesting beach. On the way back, turn left before the centre and another boardwalk takes you back down to **Foxy Beach**, with some really close views of penguins on the way. Allow an hour from here to catch your train home.

Head back along Kleintuin Road and up to the main road, turning right towards town. This time keep to the main road, passing the **Warrior Toy Museum** (15; admission R3) which you might want to visit if you remember Dinky and Matchbox toys! In Jubilee Square on the right, there's a statue of able seaman Just Nuisance. Now follow St George's Street back to the **railway station** (about **2h**).

Boulders Beach

Breakfast on the deck at Boulders Beach, available until 11.30, is memorable, with spectacular views across False Bay, whales breaching just offshore in springtime, dassies grazing, and penguins scurrying over the rocks (check beneath your car before driving off, as they sometimes shelter there).

A new and talented chef, Sean Kiely, was introducing an exciting new menu in late 2006. Szchewan peppercorn and sea salt calamari with salad, and a meze plate to suit all diets are amongst the **starters** (available lunchtime and evenings). **Mains** include sautéed tiger

> **BOULDERS BEACH RESTAURANT**
> 4 Boulders Place, Boulders Beach, Simon's Town (021 786 1758
> www.bouldersbeach.co.za
> info@bouldersbeach.co.za
> daily 08.00-21.00 (09.00 in winter)
> RR   (CC: V, MC, AM, DC)

prawns, seared ostrich fillet with wok-tossed greens, and line-caught fish of the day. There are also lighter lunch options if you make this the end point for Walk 11. It's advisable to book for dinner, and, to take full advantage, you might also want to stay overnight in the comfortable adjoining lodge, which provides an excellent base to explore Cape Point (Walk 12).

restaurants

eat

Thai seafood and butternut squash

Cook the fish in a small amount of water for 5 min or until just cooked through. Remove the fish (keeping the liquid) and divide into large flakes, removing any bones.

Heat the Thai curry sauce with the thick part of the coconut milk in a large frying pan or casserole, stirring well. Add the turmeric, fish stock and rest of the coconut milk, bring to the boil and add the squash. Simmer until the squash is *just* cooked — probably about 15 min. (You might want to start cooking a rice accompaniment before the squash is ready, as the rest of this dish doesn't take long.)

Add the prawns and flaked fish, heat through, then add the shredded greens. When these have wilted, add the juice of half a lime — or more if you want it. Check the seasoning; you may find little is needed, depending on the cooking sauce used. Just before serving, sprinkle with chopped *dhania,* and put more on the table for people to help themselves. Serve with plain boiled rice, and perhaps a green salad as well.

Ingredients (for 2 people)
1 kg butternut squash, peeled and cubed
200 g prawns, crayfish or other firm crustacean
300 g any firm fish
400 ml fish stock (kept from cooking the fish, or make with fish stock cube)
200 ml (half a jar) Thai curry cooking sauce
400 ml can coconut milk
1 tsp turmeric
Lime juice to taste
Spinach, pak choi or other green vegetable, shredded.
Fresh *dhania* (coriander) to garnish
Salt & pepper to taste

recipes

eat

No trip to Cape Town is complete without a visit to Cape Point, where the coast often justifies the name *Cabo Tormentosa* (Cape of Storms). This pleasant walk will lead you away from the tourist hordes into wilder countryside, with the chance of seeing 'big game', and ends with a bracing stretch along the coast.

cape point

WALK

Despite its name, the 'Cape of Storms' is much more sheltered, and surprisingly wild, just a short distance inland. There's magnificent scenery and often lots of wildlife here too.

It's best to get here early, before everything gets too busy: a 'Fynbos Breakfast' in the Two Oceans Restaurant (page 136) makes a great start to your walk! Watch out for baboons, which sometimes are a little too familiar with people around the car park.

The walk, signed 'Overnight Trail', begins up a flight of steps in the far corner of the car park, to the left of the restaurant. Beyond a viewpoint, the path becomes rockier, but still obvious, as it rises along a ridge. When the path becomes more obscure (**15min**), reassuring **yellow footprints**, painted on rocks, guide you at key points.

Distance: 7.5km (4.5 mi); 3h30min

Grade: rough in places, but mostly easy, with 140 m (460 ft) of ascent

Risk of vertigo: moderate — just at the start

Equipment: stout walking shoes, sunhat, suncream, warm clothing and waterproofs, water

Transport: 🚌 to Simon's Town (see Excursion 2 on page 99), then pick up one of the Rikki taxis waiting outside. The one-way fare to Cape Point costs about R85 per person (minimum of 2 passengers required; free with Cape Town Pass), plus the R35 national park entrance fee. You can book ahead (📞 021 786 2136; 072 387 4366 after hours; additional R5 booking fee). Book your return when you are dropped off. Groups should consider hiring a 7-seater microbus with driver from Cape Town through Hylton Ross Tours (📞 021 511 1784; currently R1700 up to 10 hours). 🚗 Park in large car park at the end of Cape Point road.

Refreshments: Two Oceans Restaurant (see page 136) at the start and end, otherwise none

Points of interest:
Vasco da Gama Peak (266m)
Southwestern tip of Africa
Chance of seeing seashores and seabirds

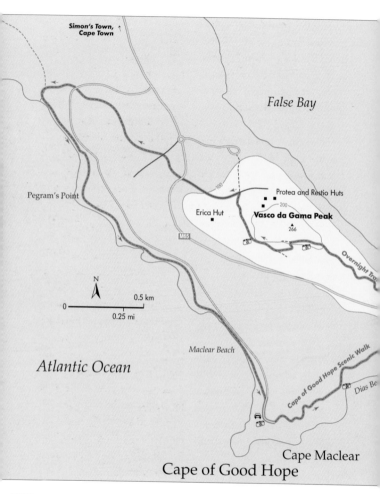

The path climbs up to the remains of an old **military fence** (**30min**), then picks its way round the left side of the hill. Vasco de Gama Peak is just above you to the right, and there's a nice view down to the Cape of Good Hope, where you'll end your walk. Just below **Vasco de Gama Peak** (**40min**), the route straight ahead is blocked off, and the path zigzags back between large boulders, marked with a profusion of cairns.

The path winds easily down the hill to a little col and meets a T-junction, where you turn right. Keep the **Erica Hut** (once a submarine lookout) to your left as you drop. The path now runs to the right of a rocky ridge, but continue straight on where a path is signed off to the right, to the Protea and Restio Huts.

When you reach the **tarmac road** (**1h**), turn left, *ignoring* the yellow footprints (which point to a much longer trail). As you walk down this road, scan the car park area below you to the right with binoculars, because bontebok antelope often gather there. Carefully cross the busy main road onto the sandy path directly opposite. Note that the large bushes beside this stretch offer the last 'convenient' shelter for quite a while! Continue straight across a rough vehicle track, pass a

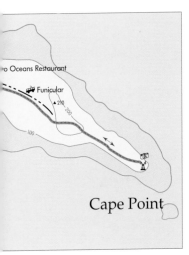

133

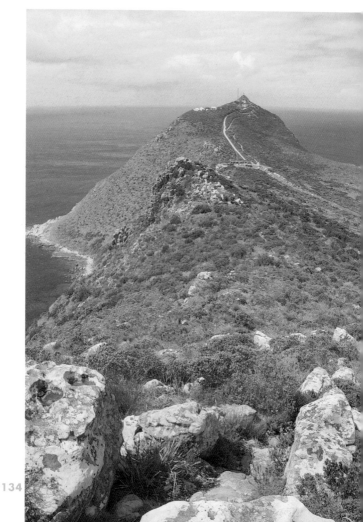

peaty pond on your left, and come to another **busy road (1h20min)**.

Follow the footprint markers straight across. (The path here can turn into a stream, so take the road if it is too wet.) Five minutes down the path, it bends sharply back on itself and down to the shore; yellow-topped posts guide your way. Turn left beside a sign pointing back to the overnight huts, and follow the sandy path along the coast. Where the path disappears in places, pick

Avocets and bontebok antelopes are among the fauna you might see on this walk.

your way over the rocky shore, or use the verge when you meet up with the road again. Keep along the shore, watching for whales, seabirds and dassies. Allow around an hour to potter along the coast (although you could do it more quickly), until you come to the large car park for the **Cape of Good Hope (2h30min)**. Stop, like everyone else, to pose for a photo beside the sign showing this as the southwesternmost point of Africa!

The stretch back now begins up a long flight of stairs off the car park, signed as the **Cape of Good Hope Scenic Walk**. It leads round the rocky point of **Cape Maclear**, across a ridge and eventually onto a well-made boardwalk. The path then heads inland, and brings you back to the **Cape Point car park (3h15min)**. If time permits, you could climb to **Cape Point and its lighthouse** (2 km return; 1h) — quicker on the funicular.

Two Oceans Restaurant

In the UK, restaurants at tourist sites are often dire, but, despite its prime location, the food at the Two Oceans is excellent (even if the name, strictly, is a misnomer — the Atlantic and Indian oceans meet at Cape Aghulas, not here).

Walk 12 begins and ends at the car park here, so if you plan it right, you can begin with an appetising *'fynbos* **breakfast'** (served until 11am), admiring the stunning view over False Bay, and be back for an early dinner before they close (it's best to avoid lunchtime when they can be packed out with tour parties).

TWO OCEANS RESTAURANT
Cape Point (021 780 9200
www.destinationrestaurants.co.za
info@two-oceans.co.za
daily 09.30–17.00 (winter) or 18.00 (summer)
RR   (CC: V, MC, AM, DC)

Starters include salads, soups and tender calamari.

Starting the day at Two Oceans, and their gemsbok fillet

restaurants
eat

There are burgers, pastas and stir-fries for a **main course**, but we particularly recommend the line-caught fish of the day (although the sauces are buttery) and the gemsbok fillet shown opposite, cooked in a black pan and served with berries and parsley crushed potatoes.

Sambals

Sambals are made from fresh grated or chopped fruit and vegetables, and are intended to eat straight away as essential accompaniments to spicy Malay curries and *bredies*. There are many versions and, once you get the idea, you can invent your own, but these are two typical ones that you will find in many Cape restaurants.

To make a *sambal*, simply grate or chop all the ingredients finely, mix together, and chill a short while before serving. For the apple *sambal*, mix the grated apple with the lemon juice immediately, to prevent it turning brown.

Another great accompaniment is sweet and sour carrots (page 73).

Ingredients (for 2 people)

Tomato and mint sambal
2 tomatoes
1 green chilli
4 or 5 fresh mint leaves
2 tbsp vinegar
Sugar to taste

Apple and dhania sambal
2 apples, peeled & grated
Juice of 1 lemon
Salt
2 cloves garlic, crushed
2 tbsp *dhania* (coriander) leaves
1 green chilli
sugar to taste

recipes

eat

EATING OUT

Sue is not a true coeliac, but is healthiest if she completely avoids gluten, cow and egg products. We're resigned to this sometimes being a struggle in restaurants back home, but most of the restaurants we visited in Cape Town (and all our recommended ones) were knowledgeable about gluten and dairy ingredients, and the staff generally knew — or were happy to find out quickly — which dishes were safe (perhaps it goes with the healthy lifestyle here). On a few occasions, Sue didn't bother to check, and meat arrived with a sauce, or a salad covered in grated cheese which wasn't listed as an ingredient on the menu — the lesson is always to *ask* when ordering.

Most places have a wide range of dishes from which to choose and are happy to adapt the recipes by leaving off sauces wherever possible. **Many African dishes are naturally gluten-free**, using **maize** *(mealie)* rather than wheat flour for thickening soups, stews and sauces, and for puddings. Ready-made *samp* and *pap* are made from maize and are gluten-free (but may contain milk).

GF, DF SHOPPING

For self-catering, the wide availability of fresh vegetables, fish and fruit means that finding gf, df ingredients for cooking main

EAT GF, DF

The Health for Life shop in Gardens Centre caters for gluten-free and many other dietary requirements.

meals is easy. We usually head for a **Pick 'n Pay** store to stock up on arriving — the one in **Gardens Centre** (the ugly tower block accessible off Orange Street, just off the bottom left of the plan inside the front cover) is convenient, and has a good selection of gf, df products. They sell soya milk, goat cheeses, rye bread, rice cakes (and the much tastier corn version), and acceptable df vegetable margarines (but read the labels — not all the varieties of individual brands are free of milk derivatives). They sell several varieties of gf pasta, some of which were fine, others not so good (very slimy!), even though they looked identical. There seem to be new products arriving all the time, so you will need to do your own research — fortunately ingredients in packaged food in South Africa are generally well-labelled.

Finding gf bread, biscuits and other snacks in Cape Town is not too hard, but, as always, it is more difficult if your diet is both gf and df. And if, like Sue, you don't eat eggs either, you may really struggle! Sue now resorts to taking a few staples with her, including gf, df bread and a buckwheat pancake mix made by Orgran (which the **Health for Life** shop in Gardens Centre sometimes stocks).

In the **'health' section in supermarkets** (usually heavily

The larger Pick n' Pay super-markets cater surprisingly well for the gf, df diet. In this section there were 10 shelves stocking everything from gf pizza base and bread mixes to corn, potato, chick pea and soya flours — and much more.

geared towards slimming products!) you can easily find raw gf ingredients like buckwheat, rice, potato, maize, millet, gram and soya flours. Sue tried some of the 'local' gf bread and pancake mixes, but they were almost inedible, stuck like glue to the non-stick tin (which we had to buy — not many apartments have bread tins!) and in no way resembled her idea of bread.

Woolworths (not the same as Woolworths in UK, more like the food section of Marks & Spencer) have several stores in and around Cape Town and are worth exploring, for goat cheeses and good quality oven-ready meat and veg meals. They have some excellent tinned gf, df curry sauces, and a hearty beef and lentil soup which is a good standby for a light meal. Health for Life on the ground floor in Gardens Centre has a range of gf and df (but rarely both) breads and biscuits, and we also found goat and soya yoghurt and goat cheese in their fridge.

The '**Health Connections**' chain (mainly wholesale, but with outlets in Pick 'n Pay and other stores) is a good starting point for more specialised dietary requirements. Check their website (www.health-connection.co.za) for a list of their products, and e-mail them for the location of their retail outlet nearest to where you're staying; they may able to order you other items in advance of your visit, but give them plenty of notice.

Depending on your dietary requirements, it may be worth contacting the manufacturers of your favourite products before leaving, to find out if they are available in Cape Town. Otherwise resign

Delicious fresh salads are on many Cape Peninsula menus, like this house salad at Two Oceans (see page 136), with grilled chicken breast, bacon and honey.

yourself to dedicating some baggage allowance on the outward journey for favourite dry products you can't do without (it leaves space for souvenirs on the way home!).

CONVERSION TABLES

Weights		Volume		Oven temperatures		
10 g	1/2 oz	15 ml	1 tbsp			gas
25 g	1 oz	55 ml	2 fl oz	°C	°F	mark
50 g	2 oz	75 ml	3 fl oz	140°C	275°F	1
110 g	4 oz	150 ml	1/4 pt	150°C	300°F	2
200 g	7 oz	275 ml	1/2 pt	170°C	325°F	3
350 g	12 oz	570 ml	1 pt	180°C	350°F	4
450 g	1 lb	1 l	1-3/4 pt	190°C	375°F	5
700 g	1 lb 8 oz	1.5 l	2-1/2 pt	200°C	400°F	6
900 g	2 lb			220°C	425°F	7
1.35 g	3 lb			230°C	430°F	8
				240°C	475°F	9

English is almost universally spoken in the Cape Town area, at least in the areas where visitors are likely to go, although you may need to familiarise yourself with local terms like 'circle' for roundabout and 'robot' for traffic lights.

Afrikaans is the first language both for white Afrikaners and of many coloureds; you will hear it spoken often, but are unlikely to need to speak it. There are also nine native African languages spoken in South Africa. Xhosa is the dominant indigenous language in the Eastern Cape, spoken by many blacks in the Cape Town area. It is polite, and appreciated, if you can offer just an occasional word in these languages. We have attempted approximate pronunciations of the Afrikaans (note that 'g' is pronounced as a hard 'ch' as in the Scottish 'loch'), but not the Xhosa which has too many sounds unfamiliar to European ears.

English	Afrikaans	Pronunciation	Xhosa
Hello	Hallo	Hal-loh	Molo
Good morning	Goeiemôre	Ch-ooee maw-reh	Bhota
Good night	Goeienag	Ch-ooee nah-ch	Rhonani
Goodbye	Tot siens	Tawt see-ens	Hama kahle*
Thank you	Dankie	Dahng-kee	Enkosi
Please	Asseblief	Ah-she-blee-eff	Nceda
Yes	Ja	Yah	Ewe
No	Nee	Neah	Hayi

*literally 'go well'

LANGUAGE

bold type: photograph; *italic type:* map (*ifc* refers to the town plan on the *inside front cover*)

INDEX

For the people of the Rainbow Nation, who had the courage to find a peaceful way.

First edition © 2007
Published by Sunflower Books
PO Box 36061, London SW7 3WS
www.sunflowerbooks.co.uk

ISBN 978-1-85691-331-7

Cover photograph: king proteas in Nursery Ravine, Table Mountain

Photographs: Michael and Sue Scott, except for page 10: Brent Best
Maps: Sunflower Books, adapted from maps of the Chief Directorate of Surveys and Mapping, South Africa (Printers' Copyright Authority 10483)
Series design: Jocelyn Lucas
Cookery editor: Marina Bayliss
A CIP catalogue record for this book is available from the British Library.
Printed and bound in Spain by Grafo Industrias Gráficas, Basauri

Before you go ...
log on to
www.sunflowerbooks.co.uk
and click on '**updates**', to see if we have been notified of any changes to the routes or restaurants.
When you return ...
do let us know if any routes have changed because of road-building, storm damage or the like. Have any of our restaurants closed — or any new ones opened *on the route of the walk*? (Not Cape Town restaurants, please; these books are not intended to be complete restaurant guides!)
Send your comments to mail@sunflowerbooks.co.uk